INTO POETRY

An approach through reading and writing

Richard Andrews

Ward Lock Educational

© Richard Andrews 1983

First published 1983
Reprinted 1988
by Ward Lock Educational Ltd
47 Marylebone Lane
London W1M 6AX

A Ling Kee Company

ISBN 0 7062 4287 4

British Library Cataloguing in Publication Data
Andrews, Richard
    Into poetry.
    1. Poetry – Analysis and appreciation
    I. Title
    808.1   PN1031

    ISBN 0-7062-4287-4

Typeset in Garamond 10 on 12 pt and 11 on 12 pt
by GRP Typesetters, Leicester
and printed in Hong Kong

Contents

Introduction for teachers

Although 'form ever follows function', this book approaches the writing of poetry through form because it is form that often presents an insurmountable hurdle to students on a course of writing and/or reading poetry. So this book addresses itself to the question 'What is a poem?' as well as to those like 'What are poems about?' and 'What are poems for?'

It seems that not only are pupils in school put off the forms of poetry, but that some student teachers and even fully-fledged teachers of English have difficulties too. The intention of this book is to make poetry both more accessible and more enjoyable in the learning community of the classroom.

Themes and feelings, or style (in the narrow sense of the word) are not the principal focus here. This is not merely an anthology or a handbook, but a series of explorations of what is distinctive about poetry.

Many of the poems included can serve as models for writing by pupils and students – not to be slavishly imitated or used as examples of 'fine writing' to emulate, but offering structures, ways of writing. It is my conviction and experience that students can better understand how a particular poem works if they have written in that form themselves. This *working* knowledge of poetry enables them to see poems from a writer's, rather than merely from a reader's point of view; such practical, first-hand acquaintance provides a solid foundation for further study and is a prerequisite for a proper conceptual grasp of the field.

In this book the poems are highlighted and the surrounding text is kept to a minimum. The poems are to be savoured as well as to get writing started. Writing that *does* emerge can usefully serve as preparation for further reading of poetry, both within and beyond the book. Interest in others' works is increased if pupils are already engaged in a similar exploration themselves: they will want to see how experienced writers solve the problems that they themselves are working on.

There is no reason why Shakespeare and Wordsworth should not enter our pupils' lives as 'other voices' rather than as awesome figures whose achievements are out of all possible reach. This book puts its readers on a level with established writers, and includes a large proportion of previously unpublished work by students – much of which has arisen from the approaches contained in the book. There is a sharing of perspective, of a task in hand, of a common aim – uniting Walter Ralegh and the sixteenth century with students from a school in Northampton, and pupils with writers all over the world.

Similarly, the range of kinds of poetry is wide: from primitive and playground chant to sophisticated sonnets; from the Third World to New York; from experimental to traditional; from domesticity to outer space; from the political to the personal; from the earliest poems to those being written today in many parts of the world.

It is essential to maintain this breadth, because much of what is taught as poetry in schools comes from the narrow English middle-class post-Romantic reflective mode, and such a narrow foundation will not support the kind of structure we want our pupils to build. This narrowness partly accounts for the general lack of interest in poetry as a mode of expression. 'Most people ignore most poetry because most poetry ignores most people,' says Adrian Mitchell, and that applies in particular to pupils in the third year of secondary schooling who notoriously turn their back on poetry as a satisfying mode of expression. They do so, I would suggest, not because poetry is intrinsically unsuitable for fourteen-year-olds, but because they have not been exposed at the right moment to the kinds of poetry that would engage their interests: poetry that is direct, free of the 'trash of metaphor' (Norman MacCaig), poetry that allows them to adjust and define the relation between themselves and the world and other people, poetry that is purely for private consumption, poetry that doesn't wear its heart on its sleeve, poetry that doesn't limit itself to traditional forms and styles.

How to use this book

The structure of the book is flexible. It falls into units which are arranged in a sequence, but which are all self-contained, enabling the teacher or student to select according to his or her needs.

Although there is a subliminal plan:

Year	Pages
1	4–36
2	37–63
3	64–99
4	100–117
5	118–133

there is nothing to stop fifth years using any of the first units, or first years using any of the units in the rest of the book. This is a source-book rather than a course-book, and assumes that the teacher will adapt it for his or her own purposes.

Introduction for students

If you are already a committed writer – and by that I mean someone who enjoys writing poetry and finds it a powerful means of expression – you will not need this book. But you might enjoy it, and it might make you into a better writer.

If you are not at all confident or happy about writing poetry, or think that you 'don't like it', then this book may well contain some surprises for you, and help you to start writing.

It won't write your poems for you. It simply provides ways of starting. Once you are engaged, once you become more confident of what poetry is and what it can do, you will come up with your own ideas and own ways of writing, and you can move on.

Many of the ideas contained here merely provide a structure for you. What you want to write within those structures will be yours, but in the end you will want to do away with the structures, and create something more completely original.

Getting your feelings into words won't be easy, but it will be satisfying.

There isn't a book that can tell you what to feel, or even tell you how to put your feelings into words. This book simply aims to show that getting started on writing poetry is easier than you think.

What is a poem?

Poems don't *have* to rhyme; they don't *have* to be about love, the seasons or despair (though many good poems are); they don't *have* to be sickly sweet, or difficult, or 'deep'.

They can be funny:

My hobby

When you spit from the twenty-sixth floor
And it floats on the breeze to the ground,
Does it fall upon hats
Or on white Persian cats
Or on heads, with a pitty-pat sound?
I used to think life was a bore,
But I don't feel that way anymore,
As I count up the hits,
As I smile as I sit,
As I spit from the twenty-sixth floor.

Shel Silverstein

or silly:

What a wonderful bird the frog are –
When he stand he sit almost;
When he hop, he fly almost.
He ain't got no sense hardly.
He ain't got no tail hardly either.
When he sit, he sit on what he ain't got almost.

Traditional

or surprising:

Roses are red
Violets are blue
Most poems rhyme
This one doesn't

They can be about anything from eating:

The green cake

This story is a long one so I'd better start it quick,
It's about a certain cake which almost made me sick.
I came in from school and put my kit behind the door.
In came my dad, tripped on a bag, and ended up in a heap on the floor.
He said 'Shift this gear right out of here
Or I'll belt yer round the ear.'
I looked at my bags, and thought a bit,
And then yelled out, 'Aha, I've got it!'
My dad said 'Don't you put them in the den.'

I said, 'Oh, I'd better think again.'
I managed to put 'em where no one could see,
And went to the table to have some tea.
My mam had baked a special cake –
By the way, my mam *can* bake –
But the cake was covered with a cloth, you see:
What sort it was really baffled me.
She said, 'The good old postie's been,
We've looked at some pictures you haven't seen.'
I said, 'What about the cake?'
'Oh,' she said, 'it's green.'
I said, 'No it's not, you're playing a trick.'
So she showed me and I was nearly sick.
It had yellow icing on the top
and dripping down the sides in great big blobs.
I took the plunge and had a bite;
Something about it wasn't right.
I said, 'What about the side effects?'
I could tell my mam was getting vexed.
She said, 'There ain't none.'
Then I noticed my brother had gone.

Keith Dearlove

to nursery schools:

First day at the nursery

The so-seemed castle had opened.
Amazed by all those unknown faces,
My stomach tightened, but had no tears.
I knew my Mum would go.
I saw Jenny, I felt gladness,
A power took us, made us all happy.

On the rocking horse I felt in charge of a
Cavalry, a leader, a master, I went fast,
I went faster.
Rolling in the mud I soon got muddy
Heavy and uncomfortable like weights, as the
mud dried.
A dreamy smell of mash and sausages, a
cradle and lullabies.

Karen Fitzgerald

They can be in long lines, as in this extract from a poem describing Manhattan in the nineteenth century as:

... superb, with tall and wonderful spires,
Rich, hemm'd thick all around with sailships and steamships – an island sixteen miles long, solid-founded,
Numberless crowded streets – high growths of iron, slender, strong, light, splendidly uprising toward clear skies;
Tide swift and ample, well-loved by me, toward sun-down,
The flowing sea-currents, the little islands, larger adjoining islands, the heights, the villas,
The countless masts, the white shore-steamers, the lighters, the ferry-boats, the black sea-steamers well-model'd;
The down-town streets, the jobbers' houses of business – the houses of business of the ship-merchants, and money brokers – the river-streets;
Immigrants arriving, fifteen or twenty thousand in a week;
The carts hauling goods – the manly race of drivers of horses – the brown-faced sailors;
The summer air, the bright sun shining, and the sailing clouds aloft;
The winter snows, the sleigh-bells – the broken ice in the river, passing along, up or down, with the flood-tide or ebb-tide;
The mechanics of the city, the masters, well-form'd, beautiful-faced, looking you straight in the eyes;
Trottoirs throng'd – vehicles – Broadway – the women – the shops and shows,
The parades, processions, bugles playing, flags flying, drums beating;
A million people – manners free and superb – open voices – hospitality – the most courageous and friendly young men;
The free city! no slaves! no owners of slaves!
The beautiful city, the city of hurried and sparkling waters! the city of spires and masts!
The city nested in bays! my city!

Walt Whitman

or in short lines:

If	Will
standing	it be
on the	the wind
edge	that
of the	decides,
cliff	or
I	me?
lost	Or
my	will
balance,	I
would	fall
I	side-
fall	ways
sea-	as
wards	I
to my	all-
death	ways
or	do?
land-	I'll
wards	wait
to the	and
fields?	see.

6

with punctuation:

The punctuation poem

He was a semi-colon cowboy,
And he swaggered down the street.
She was a definitely full-stop schoolmistress,
Prim and very neat.

And by fate they chanced to meet.

He paused and hesitated slightly,
She said emphatically, 'No!'
But a ? crept in and they thought again,
And decided to give it a go.

They joined to make one sentence,
(The semi-colon and the full-stop),
Then POW, and ! They'd fallen in love,
And then . . . .

Debbie la Haye

or without:

The ever-touring Englishmen . . .

The ever-touring Englishmen have built their bungalows
All over our sweet forest
They drive their trains with smoke
O look at them, how they talk on wires to one another
With their wires they have bound the whole world together for themselves.

Gond Indian poem

Poems can be long – very long! The longest poem in the world, the Kirghiz folk epic *Manas*, runs to half a million lines, whereas this poem is only one word long:

An unhappy bird

Bittern

In fact, there is so much variety in poetry that it would be impossible to list all the different kinds. Here are just some of them:

Poems about television
  football   love
  animals   childhood
  noses   cities
  hats   cars
  embarrassment toothpaste
  fear   death

Poems that are funny
> silly
> serious
> moving
> satirical
> depressing
> descriptive
> realistic
> political

Poems to be shouted
> whispered
> read to yourself
> looked at
> used for a purpose
> shared
> set to music
> chanted

Poems don't have to express feeling. They can just as well express a single thought:

Fresh water

They say it is very difficult
to distil sea-water into sweet.
Perhaps that's why it is so difficult
to get a refreshing drink out of old wisdom,
old truth, old teaching of any sort.

D. H. Lawrence

When you have made your own collection of poems that you like, and when you have read some of the more unusual poems in this book, ask yourself again, 'What is a poem?'

Oral poetry

'Oral' poetry is poetry that is spoken or sung, rather than written down, However, in order to reach you, the reader of this book, the following poems from the oral tradition have had to be transcribed (written down). They should be read aloud:

> If you stay to school dinners
> Better throw them aside,
> A lot of kids didn't
> A lot of kids died.
> The meat is of iron
> The spuds are of steel,
> If that don't get you
> The afters will.
>
> *Traditional*

> Please to remember
> The Fifth of November
> Gunpowder treason and plot.
> I see no reason
> Why gunpowder treason
> Should ever be forgot.
>
> *Traditional*

> I went to the pictures tomorrow
> I took a front seat at the back,
> I fell from the pit to the gallery
> And broke a front bone in my back.
> A lady she gave me some chocolate,
> I ate it and gave it her back.
> I phoned for a taxi and walked it,
> And that's why I ain't coming back.
>
> *Traditional*

> There was an old woman
> who swallowed a fly
> I don't know why
> she swallowed a fly.
> Perhaps she'll die . . .   (You can complete this one yourself)
>
> *Traditional*

How many more poems do you know off by heart?

Here is an oral poem from Malaysia:

Wind

Wind would tear a dead man's shroud
Wind as sharp as edge of spade
Wind as keen as tip of axe
Wind that swoops like bearded shot
Wind umbrella-like in form
Wind that fills the seas with bones
Wind that levels all before it

Continue this poem, or write about 'Sun' or 'Ice' or 'Rain' in the same way.

Here is another oral poem. This time it's a question-and-answer one, from India:

What is man's body?

What is man's body? It is a spark from the fire
It meets water and it is put out.
What is man's body? It is a bit of straw
It meets fire and it is burnt.
What is man's body? It is a bubble of water
Broken by the wind.

Again, try making up some questions and answers of your own. You could ask a different question, like 'What is a woman's body?' or 'What is death?' or 'What is life?' or 'What is . . . ?' – well, anything!

When you read out these poems, have one person read out the questions and another read out the answers. You don't have to stick to the same question throughout the poem. (You could also have one person write the questions and another write the answers.)

Finally, here is a poem to read out loud that is based on a kind of dance: pogoing. This is no coincidence. The rhythms of dance have always been connected with the rhythms of poetry. Poetry can be said to be words arranged in a rhythm – a rhythm that is close to song and/or dance. This poem is about a serious matter: unemployment.

Pogoing

unemployment rising
i leap up and down
suicide rising
i leap up and down
atoms splitting   rising splitting
i leap up and down   i leap up and down
parents splitting   burning splitting
i leap up and down   i leap up and down
                                            flaming snapping
tension building   i leap up and down
i leap up and down   despite it all
buildings burning   i leap up and down
i leap up and down
tension breaking   in spite of it all I
i leap up and down   leap up and leap up and
people snapping   leap up and down.
i leap up and down
                                            Phillip King

Wordplay

Soundplay

Get your tongue round these:

1 A bloke's back brake block broke
2 Can you imagine an imaginary menagerie manager imagining managing an imaginary menagerie?
3 Mister Matthew Mathers, my maths master, munches mashed marmalade muffins
4 Rubber buggy bumpers
5 United States twin-screw steel cruisers
6 You can have fried fresh fish
            fish fresh fried
            fresh fried fish
            fresh fish fried
          or fish fried fresh
7 Any noise annoys an oyster
   But a noisy noise annoys an oyster most

Which is the most difficult to say quickly? Why? Do you know any others? How difficult are they to make up?

In this poem, the endings of the words sound the same:

Have you ever seen a rabbit grab it?
Have you ever seen a turtle hurtle?
Have you ever seen a frog jog?
          a snake shake?
          a swallow follow?
          a slug hug?
          an ant pant?
        or a thrush rush?
No? Nor have I.

Lines that have the same consonantal sounds running through them are said to *alliterate*, as in:

a gaggle of geese gadding about the garden

heaving a heavy handbag hung with hasps

mixing muck with magic to make munchy miracles

never needing to know nice names

picking pieces of pie from the park pavilions

reaching recklessly for a round robin

skidding skilfully streamwards, singing songs

trying to treat tiny tots like true teammates

In the following 'alphabet poem', all the main words in each line begin with the same letter:

An Ambulance Arrived Abruptly At An Awful Accident. A Bedraggled, Bewildered and Badly Bruised Boy was Carried out Carefully and Cautiously by the Driver and Delivered to the Doctors. They Diligently Diagnosed the Damages, Ensuring that Every Effort was Exercised to Eliminate the Evidently Excruciating pain. They Found he had a Fractured Femur and Gave him Gas to alleviate his Groans. He was Hurried to Hospital and Injected for the Injuries. He was Jittery, and felt Jumbled and Jarred. They Kept him from Kicking by Lecturing him to Lie Lazily. The Matron Managed to Make him take More Mouthfuls of the Murky Medicine; Meanwhile the Nurses Nicely asked his Name and Nationality. The Orthopaedic surgeon Offered to Operate and Put some Plaster of Paris on his Painful Parts. The boy Quietened Quickly and Readily Relaxed when his Relatives Rang to Reassure him. Soon he was Strapped Strongly to a Splint, and feeling Terribly Tired was Transferred after a Time To a Unit by a Uniformed nurse. She Volunteered to Visit him. When she Went to his Ward after an X ray, the boy Yawned, and . . ZZZzzzzzzzzzzzzzzzzzzzzzzzzzzzzzzzzzzzzzzzzzzzzzzzzzzzzzzzzzzz zzzzzzzzzzzzzzzzzzzzzzzzzzzzzzzzzzzzzzzzzzzzzzzzzzzzzzzzzzzzzzzzz

Jane Bertram

Letterplay

There's plenty of fun to be had with alphabets:

An animal alphabet

Alligator, beetle, porcupine, whale,
Bobolink, panther, dragon-fly, snail,
Crocodile, monkey, buffalo, hare,
Dromedary, leopard, mud-turtle, bear,
Elephant, badger, pelican, ox,
Flying-fish, reindeer, anaconda, fox,
Guinea-pig, dolphin, antelope, goose,
Humming-bird, weasel, pickerel, moose,
Ibex, rhinoceros, owl, kangaroo,
Jackal, opossum, toad, cockatoo,
Kingfisher, peacock, anteater, bat,
Lizard, ichneumon, honey-bee, rat,
Mocking-bird, camel, grasshopper, mouse,
Nightingale, spider, cuttle-fish, grouse,
Ocelot, pheasant, wolverine, auk,
Periwinkle, ermine, katydid, hawk,
Quail, hippopotamus, armadillo, moth,
Rattlesnake, lion, woodpecker, sloth,
Salamander, goldfinch, angleworm, dog,
Tiger, flamingo, scorpion, frog,
Unicorn, ostrich, nautilus, mole,
Viper, gorilla, basilisk, sole,
Whippoorwill, beaver, centipede, fawn,
Xantho, canary, polliwog, swan,
Yellowhammer, eagle, hyena, lark,
Zebra, chameleon, butterfly, shark.

Anon.

12

Very brief thoughts on the letter M

A,b,c,d,e,
f,g,h,i,j,
k,l,n,o,p,
q,r,s,t,u,
v,w,x,y,z.

Miroslav Holub

ABC

Hay, be seedy!
He-effigy,
Hate-shy jaky
yellow man, oh peek,
you are rusty,
you've edible,
you ex-wise he!

Harry Matthews

Acrostics are poems that are made by writing a name or word down the left-hand margin of your page, and then using each letter to start your line of poetry. Here are two examples:

To the edge of the
Hedge is where I go
Everything else is

Nothing to me, my
Interest is a
Ghost which
Haunts
The edge of the hedge

Julie Nendick

Turnips
Roar
And
Carrots
Elegantly
Yell

Tracey White

In July 1969, the Apollo 9 space mission successfully landed two men on the moon: Neil Armstrong and Buzz Aldrin. The third member of crew, Michael Collins, stayed in orbit while the other two explored.

Not an earthly person by any means,
Even when back home in America.
Impossible when there's a full moon,
Looking up to trace his footsteps.

Almost lunatic with his kids, he
Races around the block like a ship in orbit,
Makes the world as small as a football, and
Sends it flying into the sun.
Tries to keep his feet on the ground but
Rarely can he manage it, especially as he's
Over the moon with the boost that
NASA gave him. He's human nevertheless,
Going grey, over forty, and waning.

Wordplay

How the gallows child remembers the names of the months

Jaguary
Cassowary
Marten
Mandril
Maybird
Coon
Shoofly
Locust
Serpent bear
Octopus
North Pole bear
Remem bear

Christian Morgenstern

Long legged Italy
Kicked poor Sicily
Right in the middle of the Mediterranean Sea.
Austria was Hungary
Took a bit of Turkey
Dipped it in Greece
Fried it in Japan
And ate it off China

Traditional

These, and other such plays on words, are possible because some words have more than one meaning. They are often the source of jokes, like:

We opened the window and influenza.

There was a man in a house and he could not get out. The only furniture was a table. He rubbed his hands until they were sore. Then he sawed the table in half. Two halves make a whole. He shouted through the hole until he was hoarse, jumped on the horse and rode away.

When is a door not a door? When it's ajar.

Can you think of any more jokes or sayings that play on words like this?

Grand scheme of emigration

The Brewers should to *Malt-a* go,
    The Loggerheads to *Scilly*,
The Quakers to the *Friendly Isles*,
    The Furriers all to *Chili*.

The little squalling, brawling brats,
    That break our nightly rest,
Should be packed off to *Baby-lon*,
    To *Lap-land*, or to *Brest*.

From *Spit-head* Cooks go o'er to *Greece;*
    And while the Miser waits
His passage to the *Guinea* coast,
    Spendthrifts are in the *Straits.*

Spinsters should to the *Needles* go,
    Wine-bibbers to *Burgundy;*
Gourmands should lunch at *Sandwich Isles,*
    Wags in the *Bay of Fun-dy.*

Musicians hasten to the *Sound,*
    The surpliced Priest to *Rome;*
While still the race of Hypocrites
    At *Cant-on* are at home.

Lovers should hasten to *Good Hope;*
    To some *Cape Horn* is pain;
Debtors should go to *Oh-i-o,*
    And Sailors to the *Main-e.*

Hie, Bachelors, to the *United States!*
    Maids, to the *Isle of Man;*
Let Gardeners go to *Botany Bay,*
    And Shoeblacks to *Japan.*

Thus, emigrants and misplaced men
    Will then no longer vex us;
And all that a'n't provided for
    Had better go to *Texas.*

That Victorian poem is based on puns, as is this joke:

Q. What do you do if you lose a hand?
A. Go to the secondhand shop.

Take a word like 'air'. How many words can you think of that start with 'air'? For example:

airbed
airbase
airborne
airfield
airletter?

You will find a dictionary useful.

If you think of all these words *literally* – that is, if you take them at their face value – they can give you ideas for writing. For example, take the word 'airfield'. We all know what an airfield is, but what is an 'air field'? It's a field of air.

What kind of farm then? An airfarm?
What can you grow on a field of air?
What grazes there?

Where is it located?
Who drives their Land Rover over it?

Questions like these can give rise to notes that are very close to poems:

Airfield

Belonging to the man
who farms heaven:
where walking is like floating
and the horses fly past
    like the wind.
Where clouds soak the grass
and birds shoot up out of the ground.
Where they can't find words
to express the smoothness
of the Land Rover's suspension . . .

Airborne

I was born in the air.
My father was the wind,
my mother was fair.
I don't know where
I was brought up, I only know
I was happy there.
I am extremely rare
and totally subject to
    the weather.

Aircraft

It has to be music,
leaving the strings at the speed of sound
and landing gently on the ear;
making the Atlantic trip
in less than a second,
sometimes at a pitch
that only dogs and humming-birds
can actually hear.

Try similar wordplays with 'earth', 'fire' and 'water'.

Shape and concrete poetry

From single words:

droppe~d~ b o r i n g

j~u~ ~m~ p   miss ng

to entire poems, shapes can be used in poetry.

pfelApfelApfelApfei
felApfelApfelApfelApfelA
felApfelApfelApfelApfelApfe
ApfelApfelApfelApfelApfelApf
pfelApfelApfelApfelApfelApfel
ApfelApfelApfelApfelApfelApfe
pfelApfelApfelApfelApfelApfelA
ApfelApfelApfelApfelApfelApfe
felApfelApfelApfelApfelApfel
pfelApfelApfelApfelApfelApf
elApfelApfelApfelWurmAp
felApfelApfelApfelApfel
ofelApfelApfelApfel
felApfelApfelA
nfelAnfel

Reinhard Döhl

Apfel = apple

(concrete poem — five diagonal "rain" columns reading downward)

1. I knew even before I opened the curtains it was raining
2. now all my plans have to be changed I suppose
3. the cycle ride is off and we cant go swimming
4. when I get used to it things will be alright
5. I think I will find a book and curl up in front of the fire

after Guillaume Apollinaire

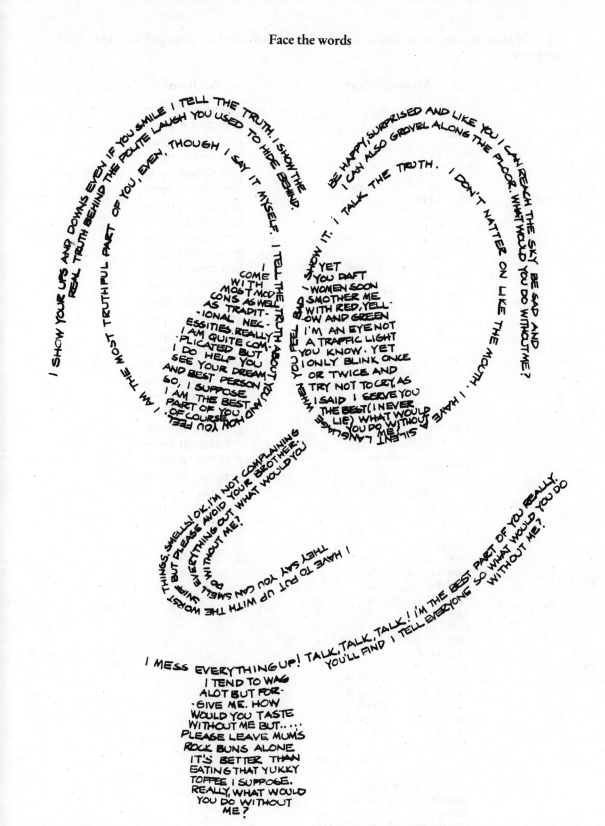

Kathryn Kent

Edwin Morgan uses the possibilities that the typewriter offers in 'Message Clear' and 'Archives':

Message clear

```
am            i
                        if
i am                    he
    he r      o
    h     ur  t
    the re        and
    he   re      and
    he re
  a           n   d
    the r       .      e
i am   r                ife
            i n
        s    ion and
i               d    i e
  am  e res ect
  am  e res ection
              o         f
    the               life
              o         f
    m  e       n
        sur e
    the           d  i e
i      s
        s   e t  and
i am the  sur      d
  a  t  res   t
              o       life
i am  he r                e
i a        ct
i      r u     n
i m  e e·     t
i          t        i e
i      s   t  and
i am th        o    th
i am  r       a
i am the  su    on
i am the  s    on
i am the  e  rect on    e if
i am   re      n    t
i am   s      a      fe
i am   s   e  n   t
i  he e        d
i  t e s    t
i     re        a d
  a  th re       a d
  a     s   t on   e
  a  t  re       a d
  a  th  r    on   e
i      resurrect
              a    life
i am       i n     life
i am   resurrection
i am the resurrection and
i am
i am the resurrection and the life
```

surd = an indefinable amount

Archives

```
generation upon
generation upon
generation upon
generation upon
generation upon
generation upon
generation upon
generation upon
generation upon
generation upon
generation upon
generation upon
generation upon
generation upon
generation upon
generation upon
generation upon
generation upon
generation upon
g neration upon
g neration up n
g nerat on up n
g nerat n up n
g nerat n p n
g erat n p n
g era n p n
g era n   n
g er  n   n
g  r  n   n
g     n   n
g     n
g
```

20

Computer poetry

headstrong	offhand	handsome	footage
headwind	underhand	handmade	footing
headrig	secondhand	handicraft	footlights
headbanger	cowhand	handy	footloose
headmaster		handle	football
headcount		handicap	footpath
header		hand-me-down	footrest
headstone		handout	foothold

How many more can you find in the dictionary? How many words like 'head', 'hand' and 'foot' might provide you with lists like these?

When you try to swop some of the endings, you come up with some surprising words:

headmade	handlights	footstrong
headicap	handloose	footcount
offhead	handpath	footicraft
underhead	handbanger	footle
secondhead	handmaster	footsome
cowhead	handwind	footwind

If you have a computer available, you might be able to programme it to make umpteen new word-combinations. All of these new words will need definitions!

Better still, you could programme the computer to write poems for you:

the a (an) this that	white black friendly angry astounded empty miserable careless	snow goat mother city life summer space wish	covers kills loves begins ends hurries forgets remembers	the	day world farm school child spring sadness hope

Try out the various sequences, and then devise programmes of your own. You don't need a computer to make this work: simply write out your programme like the one above.

Keep a record of the best lines to come out of the computer, such as:

The astounded summer ends the spring
The empty mother loves the child
The careless city forgets the child
This miserable life ends the world
That friendly goat remembers the sadness

How could you programme the computer to write more than just single lines?

Here are two dialect poems from Edwin Morgan's computer. They were compiled from lists of words from Northamptonshire and Lowland Scots dialects. Can you work out what they mean? Or *might* mean? Then try composing a similar poem in your own dialect, as if you had swallowed a dictionary of dialect words.

The computer's first dialect poems

i. *The Furze Kidder's Bating* (Northamptonshire)

Blea on the baulk the furze kidder rocked
with a bottle of flags and a budget of bent.
Sawning and soodling in a drabbled scrip
he hirpled and jolled hirkling and croodling.
Morts of mizled mouldiwarps
gaddered the ball at beavering hour
and progged the fotherer's frumitory.
His cag of stingo by the stools
was teemed by puddock, pink, and pismire.
Glabbering sturnels swopped on sprotes.
Rawky popples whewed and quawked.
Hariff and foulroyce clouted the meer.
Brustling at clink and bandy chock
his sawney doll pelted pranking.
Bating the lown with hugh icles
she pilled him on the pudgy platt
and pessed his yaum as pluft as a pooty.

A bumbarrel scrowed Joe Millar's book.

ii. *The Birkie and the Howdie* (Lowland Scots)

A dorty, vogie, chanler-chaftit birkie
brattled the aizles o the clachan chimlie,
glunched at his jaupin quaich o usquebae,
scunnered red-wud at the clarty lyart howdie
snirtlin by the ingle-neuk sae laithron and tozie,
and gied the thowless quine a blaud wi his gully
til she skrieghed like a cut-luggit houlet and dang her tassie
aff-loof at his unco doup, the glaikit tawpie.
The skellum callan goaved at her fell drumlie:
'Ye tocherless wanchancie staumrel hizzie,
ye groazlin, driddlin grumphie, ye awnie ferlie,
deil gie your kyte curmurrings o scroggy crowdie,
and bogles graizle ilka ramfeezl't hurdie
till aa your snash is steekit, ye duddie hoodie!'

–'Ach, I hae warlock-briefs, stegh the collieshangie!
Aa your ier-oes sall gang sae muckle agley
they'se turn to blitters and bauckie-birds, and in a brulzie
they'se mak their joes o taeds, aa thrang and sonsie,
snowkin in aidle whaur asks and clegs are grushie:
yon is an ourie pliskie!'
                     Wha wan the tulzie?

Riddles

In these Yugoslavian riddles printed in a book of poetic fragments the 'answer' is given as the title of each riddle. Clearly the point is not to work out the answer, but to enjoy the puzzle for itself.

Winter

No teeth, no hands, but it still bites

Snow

I flew like an eagle, fell like a king, died like
a dog

Head

Pot with seven holes
Pour water in and it doesn't run out

Corpse and Bearers

Five bodies, four souls and a hundred nails

Needle

I am young and slender
When I travel I have a tail
The further I go
The less there is of my tail
I lose it as I go
And come home tailless

Trousers

I jumped into a pit
And came out of two gates

Note that each subject – winter, snow, a needle – is imagined as something else: winter as a person or animal, the head as a pot and the needle as a creature. When you are writing your own riddles, bear this in mind – and don't make them too easy!

Here are some more Yugoslavian riddles:

The sound of a bell

I shake a tree here, but the fruit falls half-an-hour away

Sun

One plate serves the whole world

Here are some riddles for you to solve:

My first is in write but not in draw
My second is in ceiling but not in floor
My third is in cat and also in rat
My fourth is in climb but not in tree
My fifth is in catch but not in drop
My sixth is in rector but never in vicar
My last is in road and also in river
My whole is in teaching but never in learning
What am I?

Ian Parsons

There I lay, cold and lonely,
surrounded by friends who all look alike.
I know the secrets of the Great North Wind,
I have felt the tear of the biggest eye.
My birthplace is my grave.

Libby Ashurst

Can you work out to what or whom Robert Burns is addressing this poem?

HA! whare ye gaun, ye crowlan ferlie!
Your impudence protects you sairly:
I canna say but ye strunt rarely,
        Owre *gawze* and *lace*;
Tho' faith, I fear ye dine but sparely,
        On sic a place.

Ye ugly, creepan, blastet wonner,
Detested, shunn'd, by saunt an' sinner,
How daur ye set your fit upon her,
        Sae fine a *Lady*!
Gae somewhere else and seek your dinner,
        On some poor body.

Swith, in some beggar's haffet squattle;
There ye may creep, and sprawl, and sprattle,
Wi' ither kindred, jumping cattle,
        In shoals and nations;
Whare *horn* nor *bane* ne'er daur unsettle,
        Your thick plantations.

Now haud you there, ye're out o' sight,
Below the fatt'rels, snug and tight,
Na faith ye yet! ye'll no be right,
        Till ye've got on it,
The vera tapmost, towrin height
        O' *Miss's bonnet*.

My sooth! right bauld ye set your nose out,
As plump an' gray as onie grozet:
O for some rank, mercurial rozet,
        Or fell, red smeddum,
I'd gie you sic a hearty dose o't,
        Wad dress your droddum!

I wad na been surpriz'd to spy
You on an auld wife's *flainen toy*;
Or aiblins some bit duddie boy,
        On's *wylecoat*;
But Miss's fine *Lunardi*, fye!
        How daur ye do 't!

O *Jenny* dinna toss your head,
An' set your beauties a' abread!
Ye little ken what cursed speed
        The blastie's makin!
Thae *winks* and *finger-ends*, I dread,
        Are notice takin!

O wad some Pow'r the giftie gie us
To see oursels as others see us!
It wad frae monie a blunder free us
        An' foolish notion:
What airs in dress an' gait wad lea'e us,
        And ev'n Devotion!

Lists

Sei Shonagon was born over a thousand years ago. She was a lady-in-waiting at the court of the Japanese Empress, and kept a journal of her private thoughts, feelings and observations. She called this journal her 'pillow-book'.

One of the things she kept in it, apart from stories, was lists:

Elegant things

A white coat worn over a violet waistcoat.
Duck eggs.
Shaved ice mixed with liana syrup and put in
    a new silver bowl.
A rosary of rock crystal.
Wistaria blossoms. Plum blossoms covered with snow.
A pretty child eating strawberries.

Depressing things

A dog howling in the daytime.
A wickerwork fish-net in spring.
A lying-in room when the baby has died.
A cold, empty fire grate.
You've written a letter, making it as attractive as possible, and now you
    impatiently await the reply. 'Surely the postman should be here by now,'
    you think. Just then he arrives; but in his hand he carries, not a reply, but
    your own letter, unopened, but now so dirty and crumpled that even the
    address is illegible. How depressing!
To take a hot bath when you've just woken up is not only depressing; it
    actually puts you in a bad mood.
Persistent rain on the last day of the year.

Your lists will no doubt be very different from hers, and from everyone else's.

Other headings that she wrote under were:

Hateful things
Things that have lost their power
Awkward things
Things that give a hot feeling
Things that give a cold feeling
Embarrassing things
Annoying things
    ('You've sewn something in a hurry. The job seems finished, but on pulling out the
    needle you find that you have forgotten to knot the end of the thread. It is also very
    annoying to find that you have sewn something back-to-front.')
Things that you are in a hurry to see or hear
Rare things
Things that give a clean feeling
Squalid things
    ('The inside of a cat's ear. A gorilla's armpit.')

It's not difficult to make up a poem using a list. First, make a list of:

eight things that remind you of summer *or* eight people you like *or* your eight favourite foods *or* eight pleasant sounds

Then describe each item in detail:

Pleasant sounds

The rustling of leaves under the feet in woods
    and under hedges;
The crumbling of cat-ice and snow down wood-rides,
    narrow lanes and every street causeway;
Rustling through a wood or rather rushing, while the
    wind halloos in the oak-top like thunder;
The rustle of birds' wings startled from their nests
    or flying unseen into the bushes;
The whizzing of larger birds overhead in the wood,
    such as crows, puddocks, buzzards;
The trample of robins and woodlarks on the brown leaves,
    and the patter of squirrels on the green moss;
The fall of an acorn on the ground, the pattering of nuts
    on the hazel branches as they fall from ripeness;
The flirt of the groundlark's wing from the stubbles –
    how sweet such pictures on dewy mornings, when the dew
    flashes from its brown feathers!

John Clare

November

No sun – no moon!
No morn – no noon –
No dawn – no dusk – no proper time of day –
No sky – no earthly view –
No distance looking blue –
No roads – no streets – no t'other side the way –
No end to any row –
No indication where the crescents go –
No tops to any steeple –
No recognition of familiar people –
No courtesies for showing 'em –
No knowing 'em –
No travellers at all – no locomotion –
No inkling of the way – no motion –
'No go' by land or ocean –
No mail – no post –
No news from any foreign coast –
No park – no ring – no afternoon gentility –
No company – no nobility –
No warmth – no cheerfulness – no healthful ease –
No comfortable feel in any member –
No shade – no shine – no butterflies – no bees –
No fruits – no flowers – no leaves – no birds –
NO-VEMBER!

Thomas Hood

Curses, charms and spells

Curses can be single words:

> You rat!
> You dog!
> You cur!
> You cheat!
> You liar!
> You varmint!
> You little monkey!

Why are half of them animal curses? How many more can you think of?

They can be longer and more imaginative phrases:

> May the earth chase you and the sea spit you out!

> May you count your teeth in your hand!

> God give you a thousand dogs, all dumb, so you have to run around the house and bark yourself!

> God give you a gold coin weighing a ton, so you can't carry it or spend it, but have to sit beside it, begging!

They can be whole poems, like this Cherokee Indian curse:

The killer

Careful: my knife drills your soul
                listen, whatever-your-name-is
                One of the wolf people
listen   I'll grind your saliva into the earth
listen   I'll cover your bones with black flint
listen   I'll cover your bones with black feathers
listen   I'll cover your bones with black rocks
Because you're going where it's empty
                Black coffin out on the hill
listen   the black earth will hide you, will
                find you a black hut
                Out where it's dark, in that country
listen   I'm bringing a box for your bones
                A black box
                A grave with black pebbles
listen   your soul's spilling out
listen   it's blue

Write some of each kind for your friends – and enemies!

Come on, get to work you lazy good-for-nothings!
You layabouts!
You slowcoaches!
You sluggards!

Here's a poem with a purpose:

Poem to ease birth

in the house with the tortoise chair
she will give birth to the pearl
to the beautiful feather

in the house of the goddess who sits on a tortoise
she will give birth to the necklace of pearls
to the beautiful feathers we are

there she sits on the tortoise
swelling to give us birth

on your way on your way
child be on your way to me here
you whom I made new

come here child   come be pearl
be beautiful feather

Aztec poem (ENGLISH VERSION BY ANSELM HOLLO)

and this is a charm, for protection:

Amergin's charm

I am a stag:	*of seven tines,*
I am a flood:	*across a plain.*
I am a wind:	*on a deep lake*
I am a tear:	*the Sun lets fall*
I am a hawk:	*above the cliff,*
I am a thorn:	*beneath the nail,*
I am a wonder:	*among flowers,*
I am a wizard:	*who but I*

Sets the cool head aflame with smoke?

I am a spear:	*that roars for blood,*
I am a salmon:	*in a pool,*
I am a lure:	*from paradise*
I am a hill:	*where poets walk*

I am a boar:	*renowned and red*
I am a breaker:	*threatening doom*
I am a tide:	*that drags to death*
I am an infant:	*who but I*

Peeps from the unhewn dolmen arch?

I am the womb:	*of every holt,*
I am the blaze:	*on every hill*
I am the queen:	*of every hive*
I am the shield:	*for every head*
I am the grave:	*of every hope.*

Robert Graves

(RESTORED FROM MEDIEVAL IRISH AND WELSH VARIANTS)

tine: the pointed branch of an antler
dolmen: form of prehistoric arch, consisting of two short stone uprights, and one flat stone across the top

This poem is a good one to read in pairs, and you might like to record or perform it in some way.

Sounds

Get hold of some Ordnance Survey maps, or any large-scale maps of a small area, and by selecting names from it, see if you can compose a poem like this one from Scotland:

> ao! hoy! awe! ba! mey!
>
> *who saw?*
> rhu saw rum. garve saw smoo. nigg saw tain. lairg saw lagg.
> rigg saw eigg. largs saw haggs. tongue saw luss. mull saw yell.
> stoer saw strone. drem saw muck. gask saw noss. unst saw cults.
> echt saw banff. weem saw wick. trool saw twatt.
>
> *how far?*
> from largo to lunga from joppa to skibo from ratho to shona from
> ulva to minto from tinto to tolsta from soutra to marsco from
> braco to barra from alva to stobo from fogo to fada from gigha to
> gogo from kelso to stroma from hirta to spango.
>
> *what is it like there?*
> och it's freuchie, it's faifley, it's wamphray, it's frandy, it's
> sliddery.
>
> *what do you do?*
> we foindle and fungle, we bonkle and meigle and maxpoffle. we
> scotstarvit, armit, wormit, and even whifflet. we play at crosstobs,
> leuchars, gorbals, and finfan. we scavaig, and there's aye a bit of
> tilquhilly. if it's wet, treshnish and mishnish.
>
> *what is the best of the country?*
> blinkbonny! airgold! thundergay!
>
> *and the worst?*
> scrishven, shiskine, scrabster, and snizort.
>
> *listen! what's that?*
> catacol and wauchope, never heed them.
>
> *tell us about last night*
> well, we had a wee ferintosh and we lay on the quiraing. it was
> pure strontian!
>
> *but who was there?*
> petermoidart and craigenkenneth and cambusputtock and
> ecclemuchty and corriehulish and balladolly and altnacanny and
> clauchanvrechan and stronachlochan and auchenlachar and
> tighnacrankie and tilliebruaich and killieharra and invervannach
> and achnatudlem and machrishellach and inchtamurchan and
> auchterfechan and kinlochculter and ardnawhallie and
> invershuggle.
>
> *and what was the toast?*
> schiehallion! schiehallion! schiehallion!
>
> *Edwin Morgan:* CANEDOLIA

This poem, also by Edwin Morgan, *must* be read aloud:

Shaker shaken

(The first stanza is a Shaker sound-poem of 1847)

Ah pe-an t-as ke t-an te loo
O ne vas ke than sa-na was-ke
   lon ah ve shan too
Te wan-se ar ke ta-ne voo te
   lan so o-ne voo
Te on-e-wan tase va ne woo te wan-se o-ne van

Me-le wan se oo ar ke-le van te
   shom-ber on vas sa la too lar var sa
   re voo an don der on v-tar loo-cum an la voo
O be me-sum ton ton ton tol-a wac-er tol-a wac-er
   ton ton te s-er pane love ten poo

Ah pe-an t-as ke t-an tiger
O ne vas ke than tuft of was-ke
   lon ah ve shan tree
Te wan-se ar ke ta-ne voodoo
   lan se opal voo
Te on-e-wan likely va ne woo te wan-se o-ne stonework
Me-le white se oo ar ke-le van off
   shom-ber blown over sa la too lar var sa
   following an don der on opal loo-cum an la voo
O be me-sum ton ton mixed with a wac-er tol-a wac-er
   ton ton tiger pane love ten poo

That pe-an t-as saw t-an tiger
O ne vas through a tuft of was-ke
   by the ve shan tree
Nothing ar ke ta-ne voodoo
   till se opal voo
Nothing on-e-wan likely to ne woo te wan-se o-ne stonework
till a white se oo ar ke-le us off
   shom-ber blown over the la too without harm
   following an don der on opal losing our voo
O be me-sum ton ton mixed with the waters the tol-a wac-er
   ton ton tiger swam with us loved ten poo

That was when t-as saw the tiger
O ne vas through a tuft of morning-glory
   by the ve scraped tree
Nothing in the air ta-ne voodoo
   till the opal voo
Nothing seemed likely to ne woo te wan-se old stonework
till a white lot of ar ke-le us off
   shom-ber blown over the lake without harm
   following flakes on opal losing our tracks
O be me-sum and we mixed with the waters the wily waters
   till the tiger swam with us loved ten poo

That was when we saw the tiger
yawning through a tuft of morning glory
   by the well-scraped tree
Nothing in the air suggested voodoo
   till the opal fell
Nothing seemed likely to go warmer than old stonework
till a white lot of flame took us off
   suddenly blown over the lake without harm
   following flakes of opal losing our tracks
in tiger's-eyes and we mixed with the waters the wily waters
   till the tiger swam with us and loved us up

You could create a sound-poem like this by taking a short poem or a verse from a poem, and *working backwards* from it, pick out certain sounds until you are left with something like the first verse of this poem.

You might like to translate, or make your own version of Lewis Carroll's famous sound-poem:

Jabberwocky

'Twas brillig, and the slithy toves
   Did gyre and gimble in the wabe;
All mimsy were the borogoves,
   And the mome raths outgrabe.

'Beware the Jabberwock, my son!
   The jaws that bite, the claws that catch!
Beware the Jubjub bird, and shun
   The frumious Bandersnatch!'

He took his vorpal sword in hand:
   Long time the manxome foe he sought –
So rested he by the Tumtum tree,
   And stood awhile in thought.

And as in uffish thought he stood,
   The Jabberwock, with eyes of flame,
Came whiffling through the tulgey wood,
   And burbled as it came!

One, two! One, two! And through and through
   The vorpal blade went snicker-snack!
He left it dead, and with its head
   He went galumphing back.

'And hast thou slain the Jabberwock?
   Come to my arms, my beamish boy!
O frabjous day! Callooh! Callay!'
   He chortled in his joy.

'Twas brillig, and the slithy toves
   Did gyre and gimble in the wabe;
All mimsy were the borogoves,
   And the mome raths outgrabe.

Haiku

In the Japanese tradition a *haiku* is a poem of seventeen syllables, divided into lines of five, seven and five syllables each. Although you don't want to be always counting syllables as you write, this practice can provide a useful structure for you.

Run out the wrong door . . .
Come back! Walk through the other
And get to lessons!

Trevor Pye

I saw a small bird
In the green grass, it was like
A lost bit of fur.

John Hodder

My dog stops dewdrops
As they roll down the window
On his clever nose.

A. Gardner

The smell of apples
Lingers through the autumn woods
But the leaves are dead.

Beverley Tizzard

The gallows in place.
All watch with curious eyes
Then leave in silence.

Anon.

With your fists ablaze
With letters and colourful cards
Marvellous postman!

Anon.

I feel so lonely
I could happily go and
Lose myself somewhere.

Ricardo Rodriguez

It's holiday time!
Even the headmaster is
Dancing in the street.

Cherry Walker

The end of the Earth:
the last flakes of fallout dust
embrace the planet.

Derek Johnson

Working together

Poems don't always have to be written on your own; they don't have to be private. When people work together – or 'collaborate' – on a poem, the results can be powerful.

First, decide on a common theme, an idea that everyone will contribute to. It can be introduced by a line like one of the following:

> I don't believe in . . .
> I can't stand people who . . .
> I'm happiest when I . . .
> I feel bad about . . .

Second, write this in large letters at the top of a large piece of paper, and pin it up in the room.

Third, when everyone has decided what they want to say, they can add their line to the emerging poem:

> I can't stand people who look down on you,
>   as though you were an inferior species;
> who treat you as though you were mud under their feet;
> who talk loudly when quietness is called for;
> who look the other way when you see them
>   on the street;
> who have no regard for animals, and who think
>   only of themselves;
> who go on and on about their own interests,
>   and never listen to yours;
> who are intolerant, who can't stand people (!);
> who think they know everything . . .

Of course, individuals can use these ideas too.

Further ideas for ways of starting are:

> We are fed up of hearing about . . .
> We think the government should . . .
> We respect . . .
> We love to see . . .

Here is another way of collaborating. One of the forms the Japanese most enjoyed was 'linked verse', in which one person wrote a haiku, which was then added to by another person writing two lines of seven syllables each.

> *1st person:*   When I stepped outside
>   I felt the chill of winter
>   Penetrate my bones.
>
> *2nd person:*   I buttoned up my jacket
>   to cover my skeleton.

The second writer has continued the theme (idea), and also used the image of cold penetrating to the very bones to come up with the skeleton inside the jacket. Now the first person – or a third if you wish – must use those last two lines to suggest an idea for a new haiku. This haiku should develop the theme of the sequence in some way.

I buttoned up my jacket
to cover my skeleton.

1st person (or 3rd):   My poor life absent,
the afterlife no better
than the one before.

2nd or 4th person: A feeling of loneliness
No one to answer the door.

and so on: The bones dreamed of life:
of warmth, movement, happiness,
of airiness, light.

But nothing happened, nothing
came to put everything right.

You can either read these as *waka* – poems in five lines of five, seven, five, seven and seven syllables – or as a sequence that can be as long as you like.

Another way of collaborating is to write a line each, making sure that you develop the poem in some way. These poems were written using this method:

Adam and Eve

Adam and Eve had nothing to wear
So they went around all bare,
And everyone stared
'Oh how could you dare!'
'Don't you ever get cold?'
'You must be bold.'
But they carried on, unaware.

Chasing the goat

The pen has started writing.
Across the page it goes,
Scribbling as it goes,
And then it changes into a pencil
From a pencil into a rubber it changes,
And it rubs out what it just wrote.
Now that really gets my goat.

About writing poems 1

The day I wrote a poem

My mother had just dished out the bread pudding when I started telling them about the poem I'd written at school.

'Poetry, eh,' said my Dad. 'Must be taking after my side of the family, lad.'

'How d'you make that out?' Mum asked, slapping down a big wedge of pudding for him. 'Haven't noticed your family writing anything except their football coupons.'

'What about my Uncle Reg?' Dad said. 'Don't you remember his speech at my cousin Marjy's wedding?'

'Remember?' said Mum. 'I wish I could forget. Never so embarrassed in my life. Call that a speech? It was nothing but "and that reminds me of" and then a long string of stories that weren't all nice in mixed company.'

'Those were not dirty jokes if that's what you mean,' said my Dad. 'Those were witty verses he's made up himself. It's a gift with him. You'd go a long way before you found anyone else could make up a poem beginning with a young lady of Chorlton-cum-Hardy.'

They seemed to have forgotten about me so I told them that Miss Barrington had said she'd give a prize for the best poem and mine had been the best.

'Fancy that,' said Mum. 'Let's hear it, love.'

So I shut my eyes and said the poem.

'There's a stain on my bedroom ceiling
Like an old man with a beard
Or sometimes a ship
Or sometimes a cloud.
I see it when I'm going to sleep
And in the morning.'

'But it doesn't rhyme,' said my Dad.

'Poetry doesn't have to rhyme,' Mum said. 'Lots we learned at school didn't rhyme, like Friends, Romans, Country-men – and that was Shakespeare.'

'Shakespeare's different,' Dad said. 'Ordinary poetry has got to rhyme. You could easy make it rhyme, lad. Just a word here and there. After "cloud" you could have: "and that makes me proud" or something like that.'

'Why should a stain on his ceiling make the boy proud?' asked Mum. 'More likely to make him ashamed. It's three years since we had that burst in the loft and you said you'd paint that ceiling soon as the stain dried out. Nothing to be proud of.'

'I was just giving him the right idea,' said Dad. 'What I mean is – how can people tell it's meant to be poetry if it doesn't rhyme?'

'Maybe *you* can't tell,' Mum said. 'But if the teacher says it's poetry then it must be.'

'The teacher? That old bag we saw at the parents' evening?'

'Oh no, Dad,' I said. 'We've got a new one now. You'd like this one. She's got yellow hair and she wears very tight blouses.'

Dad started to laugh then but his mouth was so full of bread pudding that he kind of choked and he kept laughing and choking and shouting – 'Roll on, parents' evening.'

But my mother wasn't laughing. She said, 'Boys of ten shouldn't know what kind of blouses teachers are wearing. I'll have no more of that kind of talk. And why aren't you eating your bread pudding?'

'I'm full, Mum. Honest I am.'

'What you been stuffing yourself with?'

'Nothing, Mum.'

'Didn't you say there was a prize for this poetry? What was it?'

'A bar of chocolate.' It was no good trying to tell her lies when she had that kind of look on her face.

'And where is it?'

'I've ate it.'

Then Mum went on and on about what do we pay the rates for and making a laughing-stock of her by telling the whole school we had a stain on the ceiling; and teachers stuffing children with chocolate so they couldn't eat the good food their mother had been slaving at over the stove, and she didn't know what schools were coming to these days.

Next morning Miss Barrington called me out to the front and said, 'Did you tell your mother and father about the poem?'

'Yes, Miss.'

'Where they pleased about it?'

'I don't know, Miss.'

'Well, what did they say about it?'

Well, I couldn't tell her all that about my Dad's Uncle Reg and everything, so I just said, 'I don't know, Miss.'

She kind of pulled in a lot of air through her teeth and her blouse went so tight I thought the buttons would burst off. Then she shook her head and said, 'Yesterday I had hopes of you. I thought I saw a little spark of something. But today you're acting as stupid as all the others. Go back to your place and learn your nine times with the rest of them.'

So I did.

Stella Johns

Possible worlds

Our imagination enables us to make up 'possible worlds' different from the one we take to be the 'real' one. An American philosopher, Alvin Plantinga, calls this real world 'one among an infinite number of possible worlds'. There is a possible world, for instance, in which Adolf Hitler and not Edmund Hillary was the first man to climb Everest; a possible world in which a woman rather than a man was first to the top. There is another possible world in which Mickey Mouse becomes President of the United States, or, for that matter, Prime Minister of the United Kingdom.

But there is no possible world in which Mickey Mouse is a teacup or a football team; no possible world in which Adolf Hitler is a make of golfball or a mountain . . . or is there?

When we actually try to define what is *impossible* – as opposed to merely *improbable* – we might find ourselves in difficulty.

Is it impossible or improbable, for instance, for:

> a teacup to win Miss World
> your school to take off into space in five minutes' time
> an ant to play tennis with jam
> England to win the World Cup
> you to become a god
> you to change sex
> you to sprout wings and fly
> you to become a millionaire
> the world to end tomorrow
> astronauts to find life on other planets
> birds to become extinct
> you to suddenly grow old
> you to return to childhood
> for a book not to be a book?

How many of those are actually impossible? Is it true that 'nothing is impossible'?

I'll have the whetstone

I saw a hen lay a golden egg,
and a duck lay an atomic bomb.
I saw a toad riding to town,
I'll have the whetsone if I may.

I saw a nose reading a book.
I saw a book driving a tractor.
I saw a moth riding a scooter,
I'll have the whetstone if I may.

I saw a rope hitting a pan,
I saw a biscuit driving a van.
I'll have the whetstone if I may.

I saw a piece of mud eating a pud.
I saw a bun making a flood.
I saw a rain storm that was dry.
I'll have the whetstone if I may.

Andrew Craig

I'll have the whetstone

Hey, hey, hey, hey!
I'll have the whetstone if I may.

pickling pork I saw a dog soaking sowse,
And an ape thatching a house,
And a pudding eating a mouse.
I'll have the whetstone if I may.

cut out cloth I saw a hedgehog shape and sew,
And another bake and brew,
Scour the pots till they looked like new.
I'll have the whetstone if I may.

I saw a codfish corn sow,
And a worm a whistle blow,
And a magpie pummel a crow.
I'll have the whetstone if I may.

I saw a kipper drag a harrow,
And yet another push a barrow,
And a herring shoot an arrow.
I'll have the whetstone if I may.

I saw a wild pig faggots bind,
And a frog wool-skeins unwind,
And a toad fine mustard grind.
I'll have the whetstone if I may.

I saw a sow bear kerchiefs to wash;
weave The second had a hedge to plash;
The third went to the barn to thrash.
I'll have the whetstone if I may.

I saw an egg scoffing a pie.
Give me drink, my mouth is dry!
It's no time since I told a lie.
I'll have the whetstone if I may.

Anon.

Whetstone: A stone on which you sharpen – or 'whet' – your knife

Competitions were once held in the Lake District to see who could tell the 'tallest' story. The winner was awarded a whetstone. You might like to hold such a competition yourselves. If you can't find a whetstone, you will have to think of your own prize.

There is, of course, a possible world in which you are not at present in school working on poetry, but elsewhere doing something else:

At this moment I could be . . .

There are even further possible worlds in which you might not only be elsewhere doing something different, but you might in fact not be your present self. You might be an oar, a stone or a tree . . .

38

Everything happening at once

There are at least two ways you can write about 'everything happening at once': the poem enables you to capture several different things at the same time. One way is to think of all the things that are happening at any one *moment* in your school
in your community
in your country
in the world
in the entire universe.

Here is *one* way of doing it. Instead of four-line verses, you could just as well use a pattern of line after line in a continuous sequence, or any pattern you may prefer.

The world tonight

In San Francisco
A late nite Disco
Is getting underway
Before the day.

In Australia
A great big failure
The Prime Minister
Has gone sinister.

In Iran
There's been a ban
On school teachers
Cause they've turned to preachers.

In New York
They're cooking pork
For their lunch
Well that's my hunch.

In Leeds
The city bleeds
For the Ripper's
Attacked another stripper.

In London
Down the Tower Dungeon
The old raves
Turn in their graves.

Lenny Rhodes

The 'word' of an animal

The people of Mongolia have a kind of oral poetry they call the 'word' of something. A creature, person or thing speaks, usually about some fate that has overtaken it.

The 'word' of a wolf encircled by the hunt

I, a blue wolf,
Born on the steppes,
Had stolen and eaten someone's cattle,
And was making for a hollow,
And a place to sleep,
When the Prince of Banner,
Leading his men in wedge formation,
Riding a good horse,
Pursued me like the whirlwind.
My mortal body is a beggar's,
My native thoughts are a thief's,
My dwelling place is a hell.
What shall I do now?
The northern mountain is far off,
The plain betwixt is vast,
How I run, crossing my heels!
How the chestnut horses catch up on me!
Thanks to the dark my life is spared.
Thanks to my leaping
My life is maintained.
Thanks to my prowling
At dawn and dusk alike,
I get and eat
My food.

I have nothing to call my own.
What an unhappy fate!
I have no property to call my own.
What a miserable fate!

From long ago
I have been killing and eating
Young, new-born creatures.
Alas for those poor creatures!

Though I regret it now, it is too late.
It was fine, tasty food
to kill and eat.
And when I think of the future,
How great is my sin!
I, a poor slit-eyed wolf,
Born in a gully,
Am at my wits' end how to escape,
Scheme as I will.
Now may my lord spare me!

Translated by C. R. Bawden

The fate of the wolf in that Mongolian poem is similar to the predicament of the fox when hunted by a pack of hounds and by people on horseback:

The word of the fox

As I run breathless, tired,
Pursued by the yelp of hounds
and the bugle,
I begin to build up more
heart,
For one, maybe two miles away
lies a dense wood, in which I
may escape.
Though my joy drops
as the hounds come closer, closer,
I find myself running out
of breath, reaching out for
every burst of air.
Nobody it seemed to me cares.
Nobody is around to rescue
me,

I wonder to myself, whether to
concede my fate, for I have to
stop, . . . I must.
Suddenly a badger
crosses my path, luckily diverting
the hounds,
I halt gulp down air and
run, and run . . .
After killing the
badger, my scent is retraced.
As I come to the wood I give a
whoop of relief, only to be pounced
on by hundreds of hungry hounds.

James O'Neill

The word of the fox

As I rush through the
Coma fluffy hedges my furry legs
Turn to metal from exhaustion
The bloodthirsty yelling hounds
Travel fast behind.
Inside my head mixed
Sound and voices are whizzing round.
My paws are soaked
From the mugginess of
The grass. My droopy tongue
Hangs out the side of
My air gasping mouth.
Suddenly I see
A gap in the bushes.
I dart through the hole.
For a minute I can relax my
Tired legs and pounding head.
The hound travels fast over
Ground I better move on.
My tattered feet
And tail drag on.

Nicola Stewart

Magic words

The idea of being able to make yourself into a thing, creature, another person or even a god or a spirit has something magical about it. The Eskimos believed there was a time in history when people could actually do this:

Magic words

In the very earliest time,
when both people and animals lived on earth,
a person could become an animal if he wanted to
and an animal could become a human being.
Sometimes they were people
and sometimes animals
and there was no difference.
All people spoke the same language.
That was the time when words were like magic.
The human mind had mysterious powers.
A word spoken by chance
might have strange consequences.
It would suddenly come alive
and what people wanted to happen could happen –
all you had to do was say it.
Nobody could explain this:
That's the way it was.

Translated by Edward Field

Cheetah

I am the fastest but I can't run far at great speeds.
I prowl up to prey hidden in the long grass.
I set my target, I wait for the right moment, then I pounce.
I sprint for my prey as he tries to outrun me.

I am very lazy.
All I do is lie in the shade till I feel hungry.
Sometimes I go days without food
because I can't always catch anything.

When I have my meat I eat it as fast as possible
before the hyenas get there.
I leave scraps of meat on the bones for the vultures.
I pant a lot to cool down after my running and catch.

I feel happy but tired when I catch my target of prey.
I am happy because I know it might be my last catch for a few days.

I fear only man with his guns that can kill me at great range.
I don't fear other animals because I can easily run away from them.

David Pipes

The lizard

If on any warm day when you ramble around
Among moss and dead leaves, you should happen to see
A quick trembling thing dart and hide on the ground,
And you search in the leaves, you would uncover me.

Thomas Hardy

In flight

The sun beats down upon my head
like a soft drum,
I glide upon the wisps of air
and plummet down like a bullet
from a sniper's gun,
I dance upon the winds so soft,
so strong,
I feel the power in my wings
to fly so high to reach the moon
and touch the sky.

Jenny Wren

This dog, given a voice by Robert Burns, clearly knew his place:

I never barked when out of season,
I never bit without a reason;
I ne'er insulted weaker brother,
Nor wronged by force or fraud another.
We brutes are placed a rank below;
Happy for man could he say so.

When things come alive . . .

When things come alive and speak, there is especial excitement, because 'things' usually appear to be inanimate; that is to say, they don't have life or spirit. It is part of the writer's power to give life to the inanimate world.

The song of the smoke

I am the smoke king,
I am black.
I am swinging in the sky,
I am ringing worlds on high;
I am the thought of the throbbing mills,
I am the soul of the soul toil kills,
I am the ripple of trading rills,

Up I'm curling from the sod,
I am whirling home to God.
I am the smoke king,
I am black.

I am the smoke king,
I am black.

I am wreathing broken hearts,
I am sheathing devils' darts;
Dark inspiration of iron times,
Wedding the toil of toiling climes
Shedding the blood of bloodless crimes,

Down I lower in the blue,
Up I tower toward the true,
I am the smoke king,
I am black.

I am the smoke king,
I am black.

I am darkening with song,
I am hearkening to wrong;
I will be black as blackness can,
The blacker the mantle the mightier the man,
My purpl'ing midnights no day dawn may ban.

I am carving God in night,
I am painting hell in white.
I am the smoke king,
I am black.

I am the smoke king,
I am black.

I am cursing ruddy morn,
I am nursing hearts unborn;
Souls unto me are as mists in the night,
I whiten my blackmen, I blacken my white,
What's the hue of a hide to a man in his might!

Hail, then, grilly, grimy hands,
Sweet Christ, pity toiling lands!
Hail to the smoke king,
Hail to the black!

William DuBois

44

. . . and spirits speak

I am the god of the valley

I am the god of the valley.
I watch over the whole valley.
I had been here for millions of years
When the people came.

I allowed them to build their houses and farms
        and villages,
And live their lives;
I allowed them to build their churches and cemeteries
Where they worship and go when they die.

They built their mines and schools.
I could watch them from when they were born
Until they died.
So the valley prospered and many people
Came to live there.

But after a while I grew tired of watching the people,
So I decided to make the land grow poor
And make the mines run out of slate.

After a while it was hard for the people to live in the
        valley,
And almost all of them left.

So now there are only old people,
And when they have left or died
And all the buildings have decayed and rotted away,
I will sit and watch my peaceful valley once more.

Margaret Jay

I travel as a phantom now

I travel as a phantom now,
For people do not wish to see
In flesh and blood so bare a bough
    As nature makes of me.

And thus I visit bodiless
Strange gloomy households often at odds,
And wonder if Man's consciousness
    Was a mistake of God's.

And next I meet you, and I pause,
And think that if mistake it were,
As some have said, O then it was
    One that I can well bear!

Thomas Hardy

Another person speaking

Sometimes in speaking in a voice different from my own I am released and can say more than if I spoke directly. So although I use 'I' in the poem, the 'I' is not really me: it is another person speaking. However, I seem to get more of me into the poem that way; when the 'I' is the real me, I get tongue-tied and cannot express myself properly.

The letter

With B.E.F. June 10. Dear Wife,
(O blast this pencil. 'Ere, Bill, lend's a knife.)
I'm in the pink at present, dear.
I think the war will end this year.
We don't see much of them square-'eaded 'Uns.
We're out of harm's way, not bad fed.
I'm longing for a taste of your old buns.
(Say, Jimmie, spare's a bite of bread.)
There don't seem much to say just now.
(Yer what? Then don't, yer ruddy cow!
And give us back me cigarette!)
I'll soon be 'ome. You mustn't fret.
My feet's improvin', as I told you of.
We're out in rest now. Never fear.
(VRACH! By crumbs, but that was near.)
Mother might spare you half a sov.
Kiss Nell and Bert. When me and you –
(Eh? What the 'ell! Stand to? Stand to!
Jim, give's a hand with pack on, lad.
Guh! Christ! I'm hit. Take 'old. Aye, bad.
No, damn your iodine. Jim? 'Ere!
Write my old girl, Jim, there's a dear.)

Wilfred Owen

What might be the wife's reaction to such a letter? If she was speaking her heart to friends, or explaining the situation to her children, what would she say?

How might Jim complete the letter?

How might a German soldier write back to his family?

By writing monologues from different points of view, you can build up a comprehensive picture of an incident, event or feeling.

The next two poems were inspired by a reading of another poem by Wilfred Owen, 'Exposure', about life – and death – in the trenches in the First World War. They were written by two second-year pupils who started with an initial draft to work out their ideas, then moved on to another draft to shape their poems and focus them in more detail.

Again, they are putting themselves in the shoes of characters involved in the war, trying to *feel* what it would be like in that predicament.

1st draft

The sludge slops around the side of our boots.
Rats swim around biting us, spreading disease and death.
We cannot smell anything but death and vomit.
At first the trenches seemed secure but now they only mean death.
We cannot see for flares blinding us, weakening us.
We are deafened by cannons and bullets whistling over our heads.
Gas pours ominously out of black boxes trying to catch us asleep.
We wear gasmasks protecting us from gas and
     blocking out screams of agony, death and chaos.
We are like robots working mechanically,
     firing, killing, breathing.
Our only feelings are confusion and despair.
Our souls have gone we are but husks which were
     once men, we never retreat or advance.

2nd draft

The sludge and slime sticks to our boots,
     sucking us in;
Rats swim in the mud, eating bodies, biting,
     spreading death.
The stench of the dead and dying lingers
     around everything, like a fog.
Everything seems unreal, like a dream.
Death is merely an ending to this insanity.
Once the trenches meant security but now
     they mean death.
We are blinded by flares,
we are deafened by cannons,
our guns spit fire at an unrelenting enemy,
gas pours from bombs trying to catch us unaware.
We work mechanically, like robots, killing and being killed.
We have no feelings but confusion.
Our souls have gone long ago,
     we are husks, once men.

These drafts evolved from a poem that was handed round about life in the trenches in the First World War.

The first draft was really a brief sketch of my idea of what it would have been like in the trenches in the War.

The second draft was the same basic layout but with a few of the words changed. For example, in the second draft I missed out 'we never retreat or advance'. I missed this out because I thought that 'we are husks, once men' was a better ending for my poem. I changed and introduced lines, and in my opinion made the whole poem better. I also changed the order. One of the lines I introduced was 'our guns spit fire at an unrelenting enemy'. I put this and another line between all the lines starting with 'We' so that they weren't overpowering.

Gavin Long

1st draft

Somewhere out there are my friends, my relatives and my
    dear, dear husband.
Many days have passed since he left, leaving behind his
    wife and children.
How I long to see him, but inside I have a nagging
    feeling that he may not come home.
I dread to hear a knock on the door in case it's
    a sergeant with bad news.
The small clock by the hearth struck six, soon the large
    black bombers would come and more innocent people
    would lose their lives.
How I wish the day would come when the whole world
    will be at peace.

2nd draft

Somewhere, far away, my dear husband is fighting,
His badly scarred face watching patiently for the signs of
    the large, black bombers, waiting, swooping to kill.
Many days have passed since he left,
Leaving behind his wife and children.
The small clock by the hearth struck six,
    soon the bombers would kill more innocent people.
I long to see him again, but I somehow have a nagging feeling
    that he may not come home.

A breeze blew through the slightly opened window which made
    his rocking chair sway like it had done so many times before.
I switched on the radio for the news but was confronted with
    Churchill's voice urging the people on.
A small tear slid down my face, causing my eyes to go red.
I gazed at the large black curtains draped over the windows
    which made the room so dark.

The small gaslamp glowed in the corner of the room.
Below this lay Harry's pipe and tobacco which he had smoked
    regularly every Sunday.
Suddenly the air siren went off,
    echoing around the room.
I ran out of the door and into the beautiful fragrant garden,
    and went into the shelter for the rest of the night.

In the beginning my idea came from women on the News talking about having husbands and sons at war during the Falkland crisis. I tried to think what it would be like, and how to overcome the anguish of a parent. In my first draft I did not use much detail, but this came in the later draft. In the later draft I wrote about things that reminded me of him, like his pipe under the lamp. I described things around the house and things that happened during the war — the Second World War.

Estelle Loraine

It's a short step from a monologue of this kind (a 'monologue' is one person speaking) to dramatic monologue: the kind of writing we often find in plays:

> But I remember, when the fight was done,
> When I was dry with rage and extreme toil,
> Breathless and faint, leaning upon my sword,
> Came there a certain lord, neat, and trimly dress'd,
> Fresh as a bridegroom; and his chin, new reap'd,
> Show'd like a stubble-land at harvest-home:
> He was perfumed like a milliner,
> And 'twixt his finger and his thumb he held
> A pouncet-box, which ever and anon
> He gave his nose and took't away again;
> Who therewith angry, when it next came there,
> Took it in snuff: and still he smil'd and talk'd;
> And as the soldiers bore dead bodies by,
> He call'd them untaught knaves, unmannerly,
> To bring a slovenly unhandsome corpse
> Betwixt the wind and his nobility.
> With many holiday and lady terms
> He question'd me; among the rest, demanded
> My prisoners in your majesty's behalf.
> I then all smarting with my wounds being cold,
> To be pester'd with a popinjay,
> Out of my grief and my impatience
> Answer'd neglectingly, I know not what,
> He should, or he should not; for he made me mad
> To see him shine so brisk and smell so sweet
> And talk so like a waiting-gentlewoman
> Of guns, and drums, and wounds, – God save the
> mark! –
> And telling me the sovereign'st thing on earth
> Was parmaceti for an inward bruise;
> And that it was great pity, so it was,
> This villainous saltpetre should be digg'd
> Out of the bowels of the harmless earth,
> Which many a good tall fellow had destroy'd
> So cowardly; and but for these vile guns,
> He would himself have been a soldier.

William Shakespeare: HOTSPUR IN HENRY IV, PART I, ACT I, SC III

When you write you own monologues, remember not only to think of what your characters might be saying, but how they would say it: the kind of words, rhythm and tone of the speech used.

You will first have to think of a situation involving several characters, for example:

    a family argument
    an incident in a war
    a political crisis
    a hospital crisis

The great zoo

Strange and wonderful and disturbing things can happen when you look at the world from different points of view.

Nicolas Guillén, the Cuban poet, imagined the whole world to be a great zoo. Everything was in the zoo, from buildings to prime ministers, from stars to guitars, from happiness to loneliness, from colour to baked beans. Here are some of his captures:

Hunger

This is hunger. An animal
all fangs and eyes.
It cannot be distracted or deceived.
It is not satisfied with one meal.
It is not content
with a lunch or a dinner.
Always threatens blood.
Roars like a lion, squeezes like a boa,
thinks like a person.

The specimen before you
was captured in India (*outskirts of Bombay*),
but it exists in a more or less savage state
in many other places.

Please stand back.

Dream

This nocturnal butterfly
glides around our heads
like a buzzard above carrion.
(*The specimen
on exhibit here is the common dream.*)

But,
we expect by the year's end
or sooner, perhaps,
a select shipment of dreams,
male and female.

Five boxes of tsetse flies
were ordered the day before yesterday.

The Winds

You cannot imagine
how these winds behaved last night.
They were seen,
eyes flashing,
their tails long and rigid.

Nothing (*not prayers nor oaths*)
could turn them
from a hovel, from a lonely ship,
from a farmhouse,
from all those necessary things
that they unwittingly destroy.

They were finally brought back this morning, bound,
lingering lovers,
caught by surprise
while wandering pensively
near a field of dahlias.

(*Those over there, to the left,
asleep in their boxes.*)

Moon

A metallic mammal. Nocturnal.

Its face
appears eaten by acne.

Sputniks and sonnets.

You can create your own zoo. The poems read like the plaques on cages. Here are some ideas for exhibits in your zoo, though you may well want to make up your own:

Death	Clouds	The Queen	Tents
Marriage	Rivers	Teachers	Cookers
Happiness	Forests	Politicians	Televisions
Despair	Gardens	Children	Books
Unemployment	The sun	Skinheads	Chocolate

Death

This is death:
Something not to be tampered with.
Please do not feed,
as it could take you over.
Cancer, heart attack, brain haemorrhage
                            and rabies
are all close relations, and can be
seen farther down the road.
Death has escaped so many times
that the keepers have lost count.
It never sleeps, and never thinks.
It never moves, yet it travels
from house to house
each night,
wondering whether to strike,
or not.
It can be so big it could fill all
                            the high seas,
or so small that you could
fit it on a pin's point.
If you anger death,
death could anger you.
Death has no shape,
but you can feed him,
when he appears.
He is from everywhere,
yet is nowhere to be found.
He eats anything.

Keith Dearlove

Marriage

Have you seen these couples,
wandering around the cage like lost sheep?
They've been together now for eight long years.
First it was all white and happy, now it is
                              black and dull.

Every day the same old routine.
The same breakfast: toast.
The same dinner: beans on toast.
The same tea: egg on toast.

Their life is still ahead of them,
yet they try to escape from it.
If you just look at and listen to their habits,
you will see they are in a rut.

Tracy Radley

Jason

He refuses to believe he is in a cage.
He puts his head through the bars.
He fills his mouth with spit and shoots it far beyond the moat.
His arms reach through the steel
      to grab at people's hats
      to snatch cigarettes from mouths
      to punch passing shoulders.
Suddenly, he shimmies up a bar to the top of the cage.
He slithers through the space, body clean free of the box.
Joyfully, he runs on top of the cage, along the sides.
He even finds a way to crawl under the cage,
      into the dungeons of the ground.
Just to please his mother, he returns,
      plugging his slender body back in.
Just to remind her of the outside world,
      he grabs her from behind (she jumps from the shock),
      squeezes her until the air is gone
      tickles her relentlessly
      then tosses her into the air – catching her at the last minute.
All the while he is laughing.
All the while he is dancing.
All the while he knows he can get out.
He is twelve.

Karen Carlton

Writing from confinement is often powerful writing because the writers wish to be free from the 'prison' in which they are held, and the writing allows their minds to get free of the walls. There is a strong sense in which people who are imprisoned are not fully alive: they can't move, feel or behave in ways which most people take for granted; like blind or deaf people, they have to make do with sensing the world with those senses they still have. When they write about what they miss, they often 'see' or 'feel' it with extra clarity:

Touch

When I get out
I'm going to ask someone
   to touch me
   very gently please
   and slowly,
   touch me
   I want
   to learn again
   how life feels.

I've not been touched
for seven years
   for seven years
   I've been untouched
   out of touch
   and I've learnt
   to know now
   the meaning of
   untouchable.

Untouched – not quite
I can count the things
that have touched me

One: fists
At the beginning
   fierce mad fists
beating beating
   till I remember
   screaming
   don't touch me
   please don't touch me.

Two: paws
The first four years of paws
   every day
   patting paws, searching
   – arms up, shoes off
   legs apart –
   prodding paws, systematic
   heavy, indifferent
   probing away
   all privacy.

I don't want fists and paws
I want
   to want to be touched
   again
   and to touch.
   I want to feel alive
   again
   I want to say
   when I get out
Here I am
please touch me.

Hugh Lewin

Even though most of us will not see the inside of a prison, there are two ways in which prison life – or 'death' – are relevant to us. Firstly, we can imagine what it must be like to be in prison, especially in solitary confinement; and secondly, we may feel some sense of 'imprisonment' in our own lives and want to use writing to free ourselves from it.

Both subjects provide ample opportunity for writing of a more direct, personal kind than that suggested by the 'great zoo' poems.

Magnificently magnified

If you look at tiny objects through a microscope, they are magnified so much that they can look like something else:

a *hair* can look like a thick rope
a *speck of dust* can look like a boulder
an *insect* like a terrifying monster
an *insect's wing* like a map

What do you think these are?

Using a microscope, look at various tiny objects and write notes on what the objects *look like*, and *how you feel* when you look at them. For example:

A flea

It seems as big as a prawn or shrimp
Its eyes are like little globes sticking out
In the middle of the eye is a round blackish spot
    with a green circle round it
It seems to be wearing armour, black and polished
The hairs on its body are like swords sticking out
    in defence
I wouldn't like to think one of these was crawling
    over my skin, or nestling in my clothes!
And yet it looks quite friendly, and a little
    awkward in its splendid get-up

Now use your notes to write up what you saw and felt. Try to make your description as vivid as you can. Leave out the title and see if others in the class can *guess* what you were looking at – as if your writing was a kind of riddle.

In this poem about a cranefly, Ted Hughes *seems* to be looking through a microscope:

A cranefly in September

She is struggling through grass-mesh – not flying,
Her wide-winged, stiff, weightless basket-work of limbs
Rocking, like an antique wain, a top-heavy ceremonial cart
Across mountain summits
(Not planing over water, dipping her tail)
But blundering with long strides, long reachings, reelings
And ginger-glistening wings
From collision to collision.
Aimless in no particular direction,
Just exerting her last to escape out of the overwhelming
Of whatever it is, legs, grass,
The garden, the county, the country, the world –

Sometimes she rests long minutes in the grass forest
Like a fairytale hero, only a marvel can help her.
She cannot fathom the mystery of this forest
In which, for instance, this giant watches –
The giant who knows she cannot be helped in any way.

Her jointed bamboo fuselage,
Her lobster shoulders, and her face
Like a pinhead dragon, with its tender moustache,
And the simple colourless church windows of her wings
Will come to an end, in mid-search, quite soon.
Everything about her, every perfected vestment
Is already superfluous.
The monstrous excess of her legs and curly feet
Are a problem beyond her.
The calculus of glucose and chitin inadequate
To plot her through the infinities of the stems.

The frayed apple leaves, the grunting raven, the defunct tractor
Sunk in nettles, wait with their multiplications
Like other galaxies.
The sky's Northward September procession, the vast soft armistice,
Like an Empire on the move,
Abandons her, tinily embattled
With her cumbering limbs and cumbered brain.

Try writing about an insect as if you were looking through a microscope. Remember that from the insect's point of view, grass or hair will seem like a forest.

Similes

All the following proverbial sayings are *similes*:

> as cold as ice
> as black as coal
> as light as a feather
> as clean as a whistle
> as quick as a flash
> as hungry as a wolf
> as proud as a peacock
> as sharp as a needle
> as heavy as lead
> like a bull in a china shop
> like a cat on hot bricks

How many more can you think of?

These are all similes because they *compare* one thing to another, just as someone might say to you 'You look like you've been pulled through a hedge backwards.'

Similes are always easy to identify because they are introduced by 'like' or 'as'.

> Being stood up
> is like being the last fruit on the tree
> left to wither through the winter

> Feeling fed up
> is like being a dustbin
> that hasn't been emptied for days

> I feel as bubbly
> as a saucepan whose lid is about to fly off

The picture

The sun bears down on to a grassy hill
like a cake in a cook's oven.
The flower tosses and turns in the wind
like a boat in an ocean gale.
The leaves come streaming down
like a group of sky-divers from a plane.
The noise from a tractor interrupts the peace
like a goal scored at Wembley.
The river carries a broken branch
like the shopping crowds carry a lost little boy.
Picnickers arrive in a car, squashing life in their tracks
like a Government suppressing the people.
The birds come down from their nests to collect crumbs
like a Salvation Army collector at your door,
and darkness descends on that grassy hill
like a slowly shutting pair of curtains.
The woods become silent
like a road after a curfew in El Salvador.

The next picture is our holiday in Germany in '79.

Dean Osborne

The warm and the cold

Freezing dusk is closing
   Like a slow trap of steel
On trees and roads and hills and all
   That can no longer feel.
      But the carp is in its depth
         Like a planet in its heaven.
      And the badger in its bedding
         Like a loaf in the oven.
      And the butterfly in its mummy
         Like a viol in its case.
      And the owl in its feathers
         Like a doll in its lace.

Freezing dusk has tightened
   Like a nut screwed tight
On the starry aeroplane
   Of the soaring night.
      But the trout is in its hole
         Like a chuckle in a sleeper.
      The hare strays down the highway
         Like a root going deeper.
      The snail is dry in the outhouse
         Like a seed in a sunflower.
      The owl is pale on the gatepost
         Like a clock on its tower.

Moonlight freezes the shaggy world
   Like a mammoth of ice –
The past and the future
   Are the jaws of a steel vice.
      But the cod is in the tide-rip
         Like a key in a purse.
      The deer are on the bare-blown hill
         Like smiles on a nurse.
      The flies are behind the plaster
         Like the lost score of a jig.
      Sparrows are in the ivy-clump
         Like money in a pig.

Such a frost
   The flimsy moon
      Has lost her wits.

         A star falls.

The sweating farmers
   Turn in their sleep
      Like oxen on spits.

Ted Hughes

Metaphors

A *metaphor* is like a simile in that it compares one thing to another, but unlike a simile in that the comparison is not introduced by 'like' or 'as'.

Simile: You're like a demented parrot.

Metaphor: You are a demented parrot.

The essential metaphor in this poem by Douglas Dunn is that of the garden:

Love poem

I live in you, you live in me;
We are two gardens haunted by each other.
Sometimes I cannot find you there,
There is only the swing creaking, that you have
just left,
Or your favourite book beside the sundial.

What is the essential metaphor at the heart (that's a metaphor itself!) of the next two passages?

All the world's a stage,
And all the men and women merely players:
They have their exits and their entrances;
And one man in his time plays many parts,
His acts being seven ages. At first the infant,
Mewling and puking in the nurse's arms.
And then the whining school-boy, with his
satchel,
And shining morning face, creeping like snail
Unwilling to school. And then the lover,
Sighing like furnace, with a woeful ballad
Made to his mistress' eyebrow. Then a soldier,
Full of strange oaths, and bearded like the pard,
Jealous in honour, sudden and quick in quarrel,
Seeking the bubble reputation
Even in the cannon's mouth. And then the
justice,
In fair round belly with good capon lin'd,
With eyes severe, and beard of formal cut,
Full of wise saws and modern instances;
And so he plays his part. The sixth age shifts
Into the lean and slipper'd pantaloon,
With spectacles on nose and pouch on side,
His youthful hose well sav'd, a world too wide
For his shrunk shank; and his big manly voice,
Turning again toward childish treble, pipes
And whistles in his sound. Last scene of all,
That ends this strange eventful history,
Is second childishness and mere oblivion,
Sans teeth, sans eyes, sans taste, sans everything.

William Shakespeare: AS YOU LIKE IT, ACT II, SC VII

All the world's a stage

What is our life? A play of passion,
Our mirth the music of division.
Our mothers' wombs the tiring-houses be,
Where we are dressed for this short comedy.
Heaven the judicious sharp spectator is,
That sits and marks still who doth act amiss.
Our graves that hide us from the searching sun
Are like drawn curtains when the play is done.
Thus march we, playing, to our latest rest,
Only we die in earnest, that's no jest.

Sir Walter Ralegh

Rousseau, in his Essay on the Origin of Languages, *maintained that language itself began with metaphor: 'As emotions were the first motives which induced man to speak, his first utterances were tropes (metaphors) . . .'*

John Berger: ABOUT LOOKING

This poem was written after a visit to a dock in London's East End. It tells a true story, and is in one sense a report of an incident. But the entire poem is also metaphorical. It is about a pike, yes; but it is also about humankind – about our feelings, our sense of identity with the pike, and about predicaments that people get into, as well as pikes.

The Pike

The pike was lying there
like a whale out of water.
It had already been hunted
by the fisherman.

But now it is dying,
blood oozing out of its side.

Then it rears up
in one last fight,
but still cannot free itself
from the man-made death-trap
of rubbish and pollution.

Its shiny body glistens in the daylight
as it dies.
The area around it sounds like a graveyard.
The same deadly silence of people's souls
departing from their mortal bodies.

Then someone spots it as it dies.
It screams for help.
Steve throws a stick in
and it has one last leap
and it is free.

Then to everyone's amazement it swims,
and as it swims it says 'thank-you'.

It will live until some other hunter
decides its doom.

But the monster pike is not just the hunted.
He is also the hunter.
He attacks all the other fish
who stand in his way
to his kingdom, the basin.

Nigel Skinner

Metaphor is a highly charged kind of language. It enables you to pack a great deal of meaning into few words. It enables you to convey your feeling about something very clearly and very economically.

You will find many examples of simile and metaphor in the poems in this book.

Images

'Image' means 'picture', something from your 'imagination'. It doesn't have to be an image from fantasy. We could all conjure up a picture of the front door of our house or flat at this moment, but by no means would this be a 'fantastic' image; on the contrary, it's quite an ordinary image.

Both similes and metaphors use *images*. In the first lines of 'The Pike' on the previous page, the simile contains the image of a whale. Later, the pike gets caught in a 'death-trap' of rubbish and pollution. The rubbish and pollution would be there for you to actually see, but the death-trap is an image presented to you by the writer to help you understand the way he is seeing it. 'His *kingdom*, the basin' is another example of an image; from it, we get the feeling that the basin is huge, and that the pike rules it in the way a king rules his kingdom.

Images don't have to be *visual*. They can also be *aural* (to do with sound), *olfactory* (to do with smell), *tactile* (to do with touch), *gustatory* (to do with taste), or *kinetic* (to do with movement). Here are examples of each kind:

> *visual:* the sun seen through the branches of a tree
> *aural:* rain beating on a slate roof
> *olfactory:* the smell of fish and chips on the streets
> *tactile:* wind pounding your body
> *gustatory:* sherbert fizzing on your tongue
> *kinetic:* a leaf fluttering in the breeze

Write down some more examples for each category.

Imagery can be either 'descriptive' or 'symbolic'; that is to say, it can be used to help describe something, as in the phrase:

> The shopping crowds carry along the lost child *as a river carries a broken branch.*

or it can itself symbolize, or represent a meaning without being compared to anything else:

The sick rose

O Rose, thou art sick!
The invisible worm
That flies in the night,
In the howling storm,

Has found out thy bed
Of crimson joy:
And his dark secret love
Does thy life destroy.

William Blake

Here are a few words of advice from China on the use of imagery. The writer uses the word 'thing' to mean an 'image': something 'concrete' in a poem, something you can actually *sense* in some way.

Poetry presents the thing in order to convey the feeling. It should be precise about the thing and reticent about the feeling, for as soon as the mind regrounds and connects with the thing, the feeling shows in the words: this is how poetry enters deeply within us.

Wei T'ai

Autumn rain

The plane leaves
fall black and wet
on the lawn;

the cloud sheaves
in heaven's fields set
droop and are drawn

in falling seeds of rain;
the seed of heaven
on my face

falling – I hear again
like echoes even
that softly pace

heaven's muffled floor,
the winds that tread
out all the grain

of tears, the store
harvested
in the sheaves of pain

caught up aloft:
the sheaves of dead
men that are slain

now winnowed soft
on the floor of heaven;
manna invisible

of all the pain
here to us given;
finely divisible
falling as rain.

D. H. Lawrence

Rhyme

I think most of the stanzas and individual verse-forms (like the sonnet) are made out of combinations of the two rhymed forms that seem most natural in English — the quatrain (abab) *and the couplet* (aa).

A *quatrain* is a four-line verse or *stanza* in which the first line rhymes with the third, and the second with the fourth:

A peanut lay on a railway line	*a*
Its heart was all a-flutter	*b*
Along came Engine No. 9	*a*
Toot! toot! Peanut butter	*b*

Traditional

On the building of a new church

They built the front, upon my word,
    As fine as any abbey;
But thinking they might cheat the Lord,
    They made the back part shabby.

Anon.

Of one that had a great nose

Stand with the nose against
    the sun with open chaps,
And by thy teeth we shall discern
    what 'tis o'clock, perhaps.

George Turberville

You'll have noted that the last poem didn't rhyme *abab*; that only the second and fourth lines rhymed. And that in the second poem, 'word' and 'Lord' are rhymed, though they don't sound the same: this is known as 'eye-rhyming', because the words *look* the same. There are many other variations on the *abab* rhyme-scheme. A very common one is to rhyme *aabb* (which is, of course, two couplets):

Upon a puritanical locksmith

A zealous locksmith died of late,
And did arrive at heaven gate,
He stood without and would not knock,
Because he meant to pick the lock.

Anon.

Upon a fool

Here lieth Thom Nick's body,
Who lived a fool and died a noddy;
As for his soul ask them that can tell,
Whether fools' souls go to heaven or to hell.

Anon.

The bellows maker of Oxford

Here lieth John Cruker, a maker of bellows,
His craft's master, and king of good fellows;
Yet when he came to the hour of his death,
He that made bellows, could not make breath.

Couplets are two-line verses, and they usually rhyme:

An epitaph

I was buried near this dyke
That my friends may weep as much as they like.

William Blake

On Oliver Goldsmith

Here lies Nolly Goldsmith, for shortness called Noll,
Who wrote like an angel, but talked like poor Poll.

David Garrick

I am his Highness' dog at Kew;
Pray tell me Sir, whose dog are you?

Alexander Pope

My own epitaph

Life is a jest, and all things show it.
I thought so once; but now I know it.

John Gay

Here is a longer epitaph, made up of a sequence of couplets:

Here lies a poor woman who was always tired,
She lived in a house where no help was hired.
The last words she said were 'Dear friends, I am going
Where washing an't wanted, nor mending, nor sewing.
There all things is done exact to my wishes,
For where folk don't eat there's no washing of dishes.
In Heaven loud anthems for ever are ringing,
But having no voice, I'll keep clear of the singing.
Don't mourn for me now, don't mourn for me never;
I'm going to do nothing for ever and ever.'

Anon.

You will have fun trying to write couplets and quatrains, but you should always remember that you are in control of the poem and must choose the words that you think are right for it. Don't choose a word just because it rhymes conveniently, unless of course you want to make a joke out of it. Rhyming can enhance your poetry, but you must not allow it to take it over. Good rhyming is worth working hard to achieve.

In the staring darkness
I can hear the harshness
Of the cold wind blowing.
I am warmly clad,
And I'm very glad
That I've got a home.

Gerard Manley Hopkins

Dialect poems

The energy of poems in dialect comes from the fact that they remain close to the rhythms and sounds of the spoken voice. Linton Kwesi Johnson has said that the written form of Standard English could not free him to write what he wanted to say, and that he could only find real expression in his native Jamaican Creole:

The kind of thing that I write and the way I say it is as a result of the tension between the Jamaican Creole and Jamaican English and between those and English English. And all that, really, is the consequence of having been brought up in a colonial society and then coming over here to live and go to school in England, soon afterwards. The tension builds up. You can see it in the writing. You can hear it. And something else: my poems may look sort of flat on the page. Well, that is because they're actually oral poems, as such. They were definitely written to be read aloud, in the community.

Introduction to DREAD BEAT AND BLOOD

Sonny's lettah

(Anti-Sus poem)

Brixton Prison,
Jebb Avenue,
London SW2,
England.

Dear Mama,
Good Day.
I hope dat wen
deze few lines reach y'u,
they may find y'u in di bes' af helt.

Mama,
I really doan know how fi tell y'u dis,
cause I did mek a salim pramis
fi tek care a lickle Jim
an' try mi bes' fi look out fi him.

Mama,
Ah really did try mi bes',
but none-di-les',
mi sarry fi tell y'u seh
poor lickle Jim get arres'.

It woz di miggle a di rush howah
wen everybady jus' a hus'le an' a bus'le
fi goh home fi dem evenin' showah;
mi an' Jim stan-up
waitin' pan a bus,
nat causin' no fus',
wen all an a sudden
a police van pull-up.

64

Out jump t'ree policeman,
di 'hole a dem carryin' batan.
Dem waak straight up to mi an' Jim.
One a dem hol' an to Jim
seh him tekin him in;
Jim tell him fi let goh a him
far him noh dhu not'n,
an him naw t'ief,
nat even a but'n.
Jim start to wriggle.
Di police start to giggle.

Mama,
mek Ah tell y'u whey dem dhu to Jim;
Mama,
mek Ah tell y'u whey dem dhu to him:

dem t'ump him in him belly
an' it turn to jelly
dem lick him pan him back
an' him rib get pap
dem lick him pan him he'd
but it tuff like le'd
dem kick him in him seed
an' it started to bleed

Mama,
Ah jus' could'n' stan-up deh
an' noh dhu not'n':

soh mi jook one in him eye
an' him started to cry;
mi t'ump one in him mout'
an' him started to shout
mi kick one pan him shin
an' him started to spin
mi t'ump him pan him chin
an' him drap pan a bin

an' crash
an de'd.

Mama,
more policeman come dung
an' beat mi to di grung;
dem charge Jim fi sus;
dem charge mi fi murdah.

Mama,
doan fret,
doan get depres'
an' doun-hearted
Be af good courage
till I hear fram you.

I remain,
your son,
Sonny.

Linton Kwesi Johnson

One of the distinctive qualities of dialect verse is that because it is close to the speaking voice, it tends to be more *direct* than much poetry that is intended to be *read*. Along with the directness go a lack of imagery and an increased urgency.

Harrassment

One evening me a com from wok,
And a run fe ketch de bus,
Two police start fe run me dung,
Just fe show how me no have no luck.
Dem ketch me and start to mek a fus,
Say a long time dem a watch how me,
A heng, heng round de shop

Me say me? What? heng round shop?
From morning me da a wok.
Me only jus stop,
An if onoo tink a lie ma a tell,
Go an go ask de manager

Dem insisted I was a potential tief,
And teck me to de station,
Anyway dem sen and call me relations,
Wen dem com it was a big relief,
Fe se som one me own color,
At least who woulda talk and laugh wid me

An me still lock up in a jail,
So till me people dem insist dat
Dem go a me wok to get som proof,
The police man dem nearly hit the roof,
Because dem feel dem was so sure,
That it is me dem did have dem eyes on,
Boy, I don't know what's rong,
With this babylon man,

Dem can't tell one black man from de other one
Anyway, when we reach me wok place,
Straight away de manager recognise me face,
And we go check me card fe se me dis clock out

So me gather strength and say to de coppers,
Leggo me onoo don't know wey onoo on about,
You want fe se dem face sa dem a apologise,
But when me look pon how
Me nearly face disgrace,
It mek me want fe kus and fight,
But wey de need, in a babylon sight,
If you right you rong,
And when you rong you double rong

So me a beg onoo teck heed,
Always have a good aleby,
Because even though you innocent,
Someone always a try,
Fe mek you bid freedom goodbye

Fred Williams

This next poem should be read in a Glasgow accent:

this is thi
six a clock
news thi
man said n
thi reason
a talk wia
BBC accent
iz coz yi
widny wahnt
mi ti talk
aboot thi
trooth wia
voice lik
wanna yoo
scruff. if
a toktaboot
thi trooth
lik wanna yoo
scruff yi
widny thingk
it wuz troo.
jist wanna you
scruff tokn.
thirza right
way ti spell
ana right way
ti tok it. this
is me tokn yir
right way a
spellin. this
is ma trooth.
yooz doant no
thi trooth
yirsellz cawz
yi canny talk
right. this is
the six a clock
nyooz. belt up.

Tom Leonard

Not all dialect poems convey messages of protest, as the three printed so far do. Clearly the dialect itself is part of the protest in those poems. In the following two poems, the dialect is more an expression of local-ness. The first is in Nottinghamshire dialect, and the second in Lancashire:

The collier's wife

Somebody's knockin' at th' door
    Mother, come down an' see!
– I's think it's nobbut a beggar;
    Say I'm busy.

It's not a beggar, mother; hark
    How 'ard 'e knocks!
– Eh, tha'rt a mard-arsed kid,
    E'll gie thee socks!

Shout an' ax what 'e wants,
    I canna come down.
– 'E says, is it Arthur Holliday's?
    – Say Yes, tha clown.

'E says: Tell your mother as 'er mester's
    Got hurt i' th' pit –
What? Oh my Sirs, 'e never says that,
    That's not it!

Come out o' th' way an' let me see!
    Eh, there's no peace!
An' stop they scraightin', childt,
    Do shut thy face!

'Your mester's 'ad a accident
    An' they ta'ein' 'im i' th' ambulance
Ter Nottingham.' – Eh dear o' me,
    If 'e's not a man for mischance!

Wheer's 'e hurt this time, lad?
    – I dunna know,
They on'y towd me it wor bad –
    It would be so!

Out o' my way, childt! dear o' me, wheer
    'Ave I put 'is clean stockin's an' shirt?
Goodness knows if they'll be able
    To take off 'is pit-dirt!

An' what a moan 'e'll make! there niver
    Was such a man for a fuss
If anything ailed 'im; at any rate
    I shan't 'ave 'im to nuss.

I do 'ope as it's not so very bad!
    Eh, what a shame it seems
As some should ha'e hardly a smite o' trouble
    An' others 'as reams!

It's a shame as 'e should be knocked about
    Like this, I'm sure it is!
'E's 'ad twenty accidents, if 'e's 'ad one;
    Owt bad, an' it's his!

There's one thing, we s'll 'ave a peaceful 'ouse f'r a bit,
    Thank heaven for a peaceful house!
An' there's compensation, sin' it's accident,
    An' club-money – I won't growse.

An' a fork an' a spoon 'e'll want – an' what else?
    I s'll never catch that train!
What a traipse it is, if a man gets hurt!
    I sh'd think 'e'll get right again.

D. H. Lawrence

Mi granny

Aw luv mi owd granny – God bless her!
    Hoo's a gradely owd sooart, hoo is so!
An' thinkin' ov her maks me ponder
    O'er thoose happy days lung ago.

When aw wur a bit of a striplin'
    An' cram full o'laughter an' glee,
When aw're up to o' manner o' mischief
    An' as nowty as nowty could be.

Bless her heart! Heaw hoo had used to pet mi
    An' put up wi mi frolicsome ways,
For aw're awlus agate o' tormentin'
    An' shall be to th' eend o' mi days!

Aw'st never forget her kind actions,
    An' heaw hoo'd forgi' mi mi freaks,
Heaw hoo'd darn a great hoile i' mi breeches,
    While her apron 'ud dry mi weet cheeks.

Heaw hoo'd cram booath mi pockets wi' apples,
    An' fill booath mi honds wi' a shive,
An' hoo'd tell mi t' be good to mi mother,
    Hoo wur th' grandest owd crayther alive!

An' aw think ov her roses i' th' garden,
    Tho' it's not aboon twenty yards reaund;
But hoo'd never let e'er a one near it,
    For hoo caa'd it her own bit o' greaund.

But hoo wur no' a selfish owd crayther,
    For hoo'd luk after th' fleaurs day by day,
An' tent 'em wi' care an' wi' patience,
    An' then – why! hoo'd give 'em away!

An' neaw awm a strappin' big felly
    An' caa' in at times fur a meal;
Hoo's as kind as hoo wur twenty yer sin,
    An' as lovin' an' whoamly as weel!

Aye! aw luv her as weel neaw as ever,
    Nay! better'n ever aw think;
An' shall do awm sure, till my Granny
    Gets too near, an' faa's o'er th' graves brink!

Walter Emsley

Found poetry

The easiest way to create a poem is to find – or discover – a ready-made one that has no pretensions to being a poem, and yet has almost all the qualities you would expect to find in a poem: imagery, rhythm, 'shape'.

Here are three such 'poems'. Where do you think these were found?

1 Pots of blooming colour.
   Bring the summer indoors, and put it on your table.
   With the glow of 'Nasturtium'.

2 Phoenix, Arizona. High noon. Hoofbeats.
   You're in the front stalls at the local rodeo.
   The wild horse kicks. Dust blows. The cowboy swings on the bucking bronco.
      Silver spurs jangle. And off he falls.
   Country music plays over the loudspeakers.
   Enter the next rider. On the back of a snorting steer.
   More tumbles.
   Bull dogging. Exhibition of sharp-shooting. Displays with the lasso.

3 A half-mile walk along the sands from the thatched cottages, which are the new
      beach hotel at Mahalabalipuram, the two towers of a solitary seventh century
      temple break the surf of the Bay of Bengal.
   Behind it, in the tiny village which is now all that remains of what thirteen hundred
      years ago was a vast seaport, riotous figures in stone represent the largest and
      most elaborate monolithic carving on earth.
   Forty miles up the coast lies Madras, one of the earliest British settled citiesin
      India.
   To the south and west in Madurai, one of the seven holy cities of India, an
      extraordinary town, electric with vibrations from the caste temple whose site at
      its very centre dominates every mood and every movement of its people and the
      thousands of pilgrims teeming in its streets.

There are many different sources for finds like these. How many can you find, and how are they like, and unlike, poetry?

From the children without full stops

I got your letter and we are breaking up
I hope you are having a lovely time
In Oxford University
On Tuesday we did our school play
It's called King David but
I'm not in the play because I was chucked out
I didn't know my words
My mum says I need a holiday
And she needs one as well.

Our sport day is Friday because
Last evening it was raining
And some of the fourth year are leaving the school
I wish you could see some of us run
My sisters are very bad to me
My brother's girlfriend had a baby that means
I am the baby's uncle
I wish I knew my words because I liked the play
But I was chuck out because I never knew my words.

Princess Frederica is having a concert
We will have a crossword puzzle before
We have to finish it in half an hour
And I am in the concert and my name is Anna
The concert is boring because
We have to do it again and again
Some people have been thrown out.

Soon we are doing a performance
To mums, dad, grandad, everyone can come
It's called the Sheperd King
The King in the performance is in our class
I was an Israelite soldier
We sang a lot of songs
And did a bit of acting as well.

I like to eat a lot of things, like fish and chips
And rice and meat
School infant's play went alright
It was called Ba Ba Ya Ya
The 1st and 2nd year are doing the pipe piper
We might have a quizz
We have to finish all the paper in half an hour
And we are doing a play about leaving school
And some are going to play drums.

My best subject is maths and art and craft
We are going to break up on Friday 23rd July
And we will have our holidays until we be fourth years
I'm looking forward to the holidays
That's all I have to say, except
Remember I am Alex, Charles, Angelina, Murji
Tell your friends of us.

Sarah Jane Kayser

Ways of starting

Each of the poems in this section provides you with examples of ways of starting (and sometimes continuing) a poem.

> I once . . .
> But now I . . .
> I remember . . .

Once upon a time

I once walked the road bare feet.
Now I walk in high heeled shoes.
I cannot feel the ground under me.

I once climbed trees
That swayed with the slightest breeze
Now I climb steps
That reach to the sky.

I once ate fruit,
Fresh and pure.
But now I eat out of cans.

I once walked the night
Me and my brothers
Now I walk my room
For it is unsafe for I.

I once knew life
I now know
Life is what you make it.

Paul George

The hurricane

I can remember seeing
the little ravine like a big river.
Houses blown away.
The roof of my grandmother's house
blown away.
Mango branches, branches of trees.

I can remember seeing
my uncle carrying my cousin.
she had very bad legs
and she could not walk.

I can remember my mother
with my sister on her shoulder.
She looked so poorly
my mother thought she was dead.
People told her
to throw the dead child away.
But my mother said,
'No I will bury her after the hurricane.'

I can remember we kept going
and when we reached the next house
we stopped there.

And soon after the hurricane was over.

Yvonne Roberts

This technique of repeating an introductory phrase not only serves to get each section of the poem started, but it also sets up a rhythm that runs through the poem. Again, this kind of poetry is best read out loud.

You can choose whether to repeat the introductory phrase, or whether to confine it to the very beginning of the poem.

I'll tell you the story . . .

I'll tell you the story of how they
punished a man
He blundered and strayed away from
the plan
They wanted to kill as many as they could
This man said, 'I don't think we should.'
They picked him up just after midnight
He was afraid and tried to make flight
One man hit him on the back of the head
The man crumpled and fell down like lead
They dragged him into the back of the van
Then they drove off to the land of the dead
When the man woke he thought he was free
They dragged him from the van and
shot him in the knee
The van drove off and the men grinned in glee
More pain and sorrow to set Ireland free

Andrew Clark

Some say . . .
I say . . .

Menaphon's song

Some say love,
  Foolish love,
    Doth rule and govern all the gods:
I say love,
Inconstant love,
    Sets men's senses far at odds.
Some swear love,
Smooth-faced love,
    Is the sweetest that men can have:
I say love,
Sour love,
    Makes virtue yield as beauty's slave.
A bitter sweet, a folly worst of all
That forceth wisdom to be folly's thrall.

Love is sweet,
Wherein sweet;
    In fading pleasures that do pain.
Beauty sweet.
Is that sweet,
    That yieldeth sorrow for a gain?
If love's sweet,
Herein sweet,
    That minute's joys are monthly woes.
'Tis not sweet,
That is sweet
    Nowhere, but where repentance grows.
Then love who list, if beauty be so sour:
Labour for me; love rest in prince's bower.

Robert Greene: MENAPHON

What is . . . ?
Come on, tell us . . .

A description of love

Now what is love? I pray thee, tell.
It is that fountain and that well,
Where pleasure and repentance dwell.
It is perhaps that sauncing bell,
That tolls all in to heaven or hell:
And this is love, as I hear tell.

Yet what is love? I pray thee say.
It is a work on holy-day;
It is December matched with May;
When lusty bloods, in fresh array,
Hear ten months after of the play:
And this is love, as I hear say.

Yet what is love? I pray thee sayn.
It is a sunshine mixed with rain;
It is a tooth-ache, or like pain;
It is a game where none doth gain;
The lass saith no, and would full fain:
And this is love, as I hear sayn.

Yet what is love? I pray thee say.
It is a yea, it is a nay,
A pretty kind of sporting fray;
It is a thing will soon away;
Then take the vantage while you may:
And this is love, as I hear say.

Yet what is love? I pray thee show.
A thing that creeps, it cannot go;
A prize that passeth to and fro;
A thing for one, a thing for mo;
And he that proves must find it so:
And this is love, sweet friend, I trow.

Sir Walter Ralegh

sauncing bell: a bell rung during mass

The technique of using a repeated phrase to start the writing of a poem has been used by Kenneth Koch in New York City schools. Here is some of the work of his students.

I seem to be . . . but I really am . . .

My friends think I'm not equal
But I know I'm as good
My friends think that I'm not as smart as them
But I know I am.
Everybody thinks I hate cities
But I couldn't live on a farm
My parents think I hate my brother
But I couldn't do without him
Some think I can't run as fast or throw as far
But I know I can
Most people do not think I am an animal lover
But that is what has kept me up
My brother and sister don't think I will succeed
But I know I will.
Most people think if one of my friends is gone he's gone
But really my best friend saves me every time he talks.
Most people just think that I think the situation is bad
But I know it's horrible.
Many think I don't care
But really I want the world to be one family.

Jeff Morley

I seem to be but I am a . . .

I seem to be a man in the flying trapeze. But I am a man in
    the garbage can.
I seem to be an eagle taking a path of clouds. But I am a devil
    taking baths of fire.
I seem to be a crocodile. But I'm a fish being stretched in a
    whale.
I seem to be a man diving in the water. But I'm a gorilla
    swinging from a tree.
I seem to be a pretty color. But I am a word that means gone,
    that word is: The End.

José Lopez

Other 'ways of starting' are:

Sometimes I wish . . .
I can't forget . . .
You'll never believe this, but . . .
Look at the way they . . .

You can either use them to start every line, or simply have them start the poem.

Action replay

Think of a very simple action, like waking up or striking a match. Write it down.

> I wake up

Now start again, but make it *two* short lines:

> I open my eyes
> and wake up

Then make it four:

> I turn over
> rub the sleep
> from my eyes
> and wake up

Double the number of lines again, but still keep to the simple action of waking up:

> I turn over
> stretch my legs
> curl up again
> in the warmth
> rub the sleep
> from my eyes
> and reluctantly
> I wake up

Now make it sixteen lines. Don't move beyond the simple action you started with:

> I turn over
> in my large bed
> stretch my legs
> that feel like logs
> curl up again in the warmth
> and sink back into sleep
> into the deep sheets
> but I must wake up
> I rub the sleep
> from my eyes
> and reluctantly
> shuffle to the edge of the bed
> and then I open my eyes
> without seeing much
> I feel very tired
> but I wake up

Now try 32 lines; and 64, 128, 256 . . .

These are 'action replays' of waking up at increasingly slow speeds. The point is that each time you double the number of lines, you are increasing the detail, as if you were magnifying the action. You have to think hard to break down the action into as many 'frames' as you can.

On the next page you'll find a completed poem.

I pick up my knife and fork

I pick up my knife and fork.

With great anticipation,
I pick up my knife and fork.

My stomach calls,
And my nose excites my palate,
As with great anticipation,
I pick up my knife and fork.

The food arrives at the table,
My eyes are amazed,
But then I see butter beans,
And Yorkshire pudding – what a feast!
My stomach calls,
And my nose excites my palate,
As with great anticipation,
I pick up my knife and fork.

My hands tremble,
The steam rises in my face.
The smell wafts towards me,
My mouth waters and the saliva forms.
The food fascinates my eyes,
I am spellbound by the scene.
I go and sit down,
I wait. Suddenly,
The food arrives at the table,
My eyes are amazed,
But then I see butter beans,
And Yorkshire pudding – what a feast!
My stomach calls,
And my nose excites my palate,
As with great anticipation,
I pick up my knife and fork.

Craig Turnock

Notice that Craig has 'built on to' his poem, repeating what he has already written; and that the repetition sets up a feeling of expectation and suspense that is very appropriate to the subject of the poem.

Other subjects for this kind of treatment might be:

waiting for a result of some kind
waiting for your name to be called out for some reason
waiting for a declaration of war
waiting for important news

Instamatic

Imagine you had an instamatic camera, and could take photographs of particular moments that can only be caught on film.

Moscow, 1st August 1980

Washington, 30th March 1981

Use the photographs above – or your own idea – and write an 'instamatic poem' yourself. But instead of a camera, all you have are words. Your eyes are the camera, your brain the film, and your paper the print.

Glasgow 5 March 1971

With a ragged diamond
of shattered plate-glass
a young man and his girl
are falling backwards into a shop-window.
The young man's face
is bristling with fragments of glass
and the girl's leg has caught
on the broken window
and spurts arterial blood
over her wet-look white coat.
Their arms are starfished out
braced for impact,
their faces show surprise, shock,
and the beginning of pain.
The two youths who have pushed them
are about to complete the operation
reaching into the window
to loot what they can smartly.
Their faces show no expression.
It is a sharp clear night
in Sauchiehall Street.
In the background two drivers
keep their eyes on the road.

Edwin Morgan

Fallin Stirlingshire October 1970

A man has thrown his collie into the dustbin
outside his house. The dog
has been struck by a car.
He glances briefly into the bin
before he bangs down the lid:
the animal is whimpering and scuffling, already
it has half sunk into the ashes.
In the background the man's wife
looks coldly from the window, approving.

Innsbruck July 1971

A furious baker with wasps in his pastry
has sucked a swarm of them into the bag
of a vacuum-cleaner and fixed the bag
to a gas-pipe. But in this picture
the bag has just burst, and the man is falling
backwards black with clouds of stings.
The furious wasps have a baker in their pastry.

Edwin Morgan

Backwards

Have you ever seen a film sequence backwards?

What else would look funny or interesting when seen in reverse? Things like:
someone eating?
someone jumping off a cliff?
running?
a chimney stack being demolished?

American planes, full of holes and wounded men and corpses took off backwards
from an airfield in England. Over France, a few German fighter planes flew at them
backwards, sucked bullets and shell fragments from some of the planes and crewmen.
They did the same for wrecked American bombers on the ground, and those planes
flew up backwards to join the formation.

The formation flew backwards over a German city that was in flames. The bombers
opened their bomb bay doors, exerted a miraculous magnetism which shrunk the
fires, gathered them into cylindrical steel containers, and lifted the containers into the
bellies of the planes. The containers were stored neatly in racks. The Germans below
had miraculous devices of their own, which were long steel tubes. They used them to
suck more fragments from the crewmen and planes. But there were still a few
wounded Americans, though, and some of the bombers were in bad repair. Over
France, though, German fighters came up again, made everything and everybody as
good as new.

Kurt Vonnegut: SLAUGHTERHOUSE FIVE

Film put in backwards

When I woke
I woke in the breathless black
Of the box.
     I heard: the earth
Was opening over me. Clods
Fluttered back
     To the shovel. The
Dear box, with me the dear
     Departed, gently rose.
The lid flew up and I
Stood, feeling:
     Three bullets travel
Out of my chest
Into the rifles of soldiers, who
     Marched off, gasping
Out of the air a song
With calm firm steps
     Backwards.

Günter Kunert
(translated by Christopher Middleton)

Have you ever seen film running backwards? Can you give any examples of actions which you have seen running backwards? Which are the funniest, or strangest?

A birth backwards

The baby lies there on his back.
The umbilical cord is put together.
The mother is waiting for the moment
   when the baby's life will change
   from one of light to one of darkness.
The doctors, who are now so used to doing this,
   get ready.
The father is there at the mother's side:
   they have been waiting a long time for this day.
The doctor lifts up the after-birth.
The after-birth is in alright.
The baby starts to cry – this is a very good sign.
The child is a breach so the head goes in first.
Then the rest of the little body,
   and finally the feet.
Everyone is happy, but it is painful for the mother.
But the baby will get smaller and smaller
   and less like the child we know week by week.
Soon it will be an egg,
   and that too will disappear.
The mother goes home feeling very happy.

Rachel Hutton

Storytelling in verse

A note or Something for Bruce

Did I tell you about the saxophonist
who was playing in a rock band
and who, on reaching a certain note
in their penultimate number
kept on playing that same note
and seemed to find unlimited breath for it
because he loved it so much;
and who, because he could not move
   off this one note,
sent the rest of the band into total confusion
– a confusion of fingers and strings
and hair and sequins and things –
so eventually they had to unplug their instruments
and unravel themselves and leave him to it?
Meanwhile the audience were wondering
whether to clap or not, and finally
got up noisily from their seats and left
amid tumultuous coughing and complaining.
Which left the saxophonist on stage
playing this wonderful note
and looking to all intents and purposes
as if he would never stop playing it.

That's what the caretaker thought, anyway,
who at midnight switched all the lights off
and carried the saxophonist offstage, still playing,
and put him in a taxi home
(though the driver shut the window between them)
and finally got him to bed,
still playing that same note.
His neighbours weren't very pleased.

Note:
Three years later and he's still playing it! He has a few
problems eating and so forth, but he has got into the
Guinness Book of Records. An American composer
called Lamont Purcell has adopted the note and
called it 'Non-variations on a note by Splikowski' or
'Something for Bruce'.

   Poetry allows you to tell a short story concisely and with a rhythm usually employed by
story*tellers*. The story told here would probably be thought too short for a telling in prose, but it
does have a clear beginning, middle and end.
   Notice that the writer has only rhymed once in the whole poem; that the rest of the poem is in
blank verse (lines of a roughly equal length without rhyme). The footnote is in prose to indicate a
change in the style of reading at the end: it's more factual, dry and tongue-in-cheek.

The next poem (written by an Eskimo) is in a similar style, but its subject-matter and tone are completely different:

The invisible men

There is a tribe of invisible men
who move around us like shadows – have you felt them?
They have bodies like ours and live just like us,
using the same kind of weapons and tools.
You can see their tracks in the snow sometimes
and even their igloos
but never the invisible men themselves.
They cannot be seen except when they die
for then they become visible.

It once happened that a human woman
married one of the invisible men.
He was a good husband in every way:
He went out hunting and brought her food,
and they could talk together like any other couple.
But the wife could not bear the thought
that she did not know what the man she married looked like.
One day when they were both at home
she was so overcome with curiosity to see him
that she stabbed with a knife where she knew he was sitting.
And her desire was fulfilled:
Before her eyes a handsome young man fell to the floor.
But he was cold and dead, and too late
she realized what she had done,
and sobbed her heart out.

When the invisible men heard about this murder
they came out of their igloos to take revenge.
Their bows were seen moving through the air
and the bow strings stretching as they aimed their arrows.
The humans stood there helplessly
for they had no idea what to do or how to fight
because they could not see their assailants.
But the invisible men had a code of honor
that forbade them to attack opponents
who could not defend themselves,
so they did not let their arrows fly,
and nothing happened; there was no battle after all
and everyone went back to their ordinary lives.

Nakasuk
(translated by Knud Rasmussen and this final version by Edward Field)

84

This story is narrated by a woman. It is more a series of reflections than a sequence of events:

The medal

When the telegram arrived
I was combing my hair in the sun
And gossiping with the servants.
It said the Government were sorry
My husband was dead, killed in action.
For two days I did not know
What had happened. Then I woke
To mother's voice in the next room
Comforting a weeping neighbour
(As if she were the bereaved one).
Slowly, full consciousness returned.
I dressed for the first time as a widow.
I ate my first meal as a widow.
When I was resigned to thinking of him
As lying scattered in a rice-field,
A thighbone here, a breastbone there,
The rest gifted to the vultures,
They printed his name in the papers,
And a photograph of his bachelor days.
He had died a hero.
The friends trooped in again
This time to congratulate.
I heard my father accepting
The tributes with a tired mouth.
I was invited to the ceremony
Where the general gave me a medal
And patted my son on the head.
For an entire week the little fellow
Strutted around the bazaar
With the medal pinned on his shirt,
And the neighbours gave him sweets.
Now the medal is lying in its box
And is taken out less and less.
What shall I do with it?
A medal has no hands, no lips, no genitals.
It is exactly what it looks like:
Just another piece of bronze.

Taufiq Rafat

The following lines are taken from the beginning of a long narrative poem by Wordsworth, about an old shepherd in the Lake District:

> Upon the Forest-side in Grasmere Vale
> There dwelt a shepherd, Michael was his name,
> An old man, stout of heart, and strong of limb.
> His bodily frame had been from youth to age
> Of an unusual strength: his mind was keen,
> Intense and frugal, apt for all affairs,
> And in his shepherd's calling he was prompt
> And watchful more than ordinary men . . .

Again, note that the writer uses a long line to tell the story – a line which gives him enough room to tell it. Again, there is no rhyme; if he had chosen to tell the story in rhyming couplets, for example, it might well have had a restraining effect on the movement and momentum of the story itself.

But there is a more definite rhythm to this extract. Read all the poems in this section aloud and try to identify the differences in their rhythms.

You may like to try telling a story in verse, perhaps using a story that you have already told or written elsewhere. If you are stuck for a theme, begin as Taufiq Rafat begins, 'When the telegram arrived . . .'

A *ballad* was originally a song meant to go with a dance, often celebrating or attacking certain people, institutions or ideas. The more modern sense is of a spirited poem in short stanzas telling a story. These should be read out, or even better, sung.

Sir John Barleycorn

> There came three men from out of the west
> Their victory to try;
> And they have ta'en a solemn oath,
> Poor Barleycorn should die.
>
> They took a plough and ploughed him in,
> Clods harrowed on his head;
> And then they took a solemn oath
> John Barleycorn was dead.
>
> There he lay sleeping in the ground
> Till rain on him did fall;
> Then Barleycorn sprung up his head,
> And so amazed them all.
>
> There he remained till Midsummer
> And look'd both pale and wan;
> Then Barleycorn he got a beard
> And so became a man.
>
> Then they sent men with scythes so sharp
> To cut him off at knee;
> And then poor Johny Barleycorn
> They served most barbarouslie.

Then they sent men with pitchforks strong
To pierce him through the heart;
And like a doleful Tragedy
They bound him in a cart.

And then they brought him to a barn
A prisoner to endure;
And so they fetched him out again,
And laid him on the floor.

Then they set men with holly clubs,
To beat the flesh from th' bones;
But the miller served him worse than that,
He ground him 'twixt two stones.

O! Barleycorn is the choicest grain
That e'er was sown on land:
It will do more than any grain
By the turning of your hand.

It will make a boy into a man,
A man into an ass:
To silver it will change your gold,
Your silver into brass.

It will make the huntsman hunt the fox,
That never wound a horn;
It will bring the tinker to the stocks
That people may him scorn.

O! Barleycorn is the choicest grain
That e'er was sown on land.
And it will cause a man to drink
Till he neither can go nor stand.

Traditional

Observing creatures

Writing descriptions of things you have observed – or are observing – is not always as easy as it may sound. Before you start writing, you've got to *look* very closely.

Good watchers are invisible: they either hide themselves or keep very still. Even so, sometimes the object of your observation flies off, or runs off, or disappears. Then you either have to find it again, or use your memory to recall the details you need for your description.

stumps

snails

Blackbirds and thrushes particularly the former feed in hard winters upon the shell snail horns by hunting them from the hedge bottoms and wood stulps and taking them to a stone where they break them in a very dextrous manner. Any curious observer of nature may see in hard frosts the shells of pootys thickly littered round a stone in the lanes. And if he waits a short time he will quickly see one of these birds coming with a snailhorn in his bill which he constantly taps on a stone until it is broken. He then extracts the snail and like a true sportsman eagerly hastens to hunt them again in the hedges or woods where a frequent rustle of their little feet is heard among the dead leaves.

John Clare

If you are observing birds, you must be particularly skilful:

Bird watching

Before we got to the Railway we heard a robin then another came and in the end there were three. Then we came to twelve blackbirds on a football field and also a song thrush feeding. Next we saw about 5 black headed gulls in fact they are the smallest gulls in britain in summer they have a chocolatey head and in winter they have a white head with a black spot behind the eye then we saw a bluetit flying towards us then on the other side of the road we saw a great tit. The great tits have like a black cap and beard which goes between its legs up to its tail and has white cheeks and a yellow waistcoat and brown wings and a brown tail then suddenly we saw a small brown bird with like a stub as a tail it was a wren then we saw a blackbird's nest with inter twining twigs, feathers leaves then overhead we saw two wood pigeons fly over then we saw a chaffinch female she had a brown body with a black tail with white feathers at each side. Next we saw a hedge sparrow it was brown and very dark brown in stripes next we saw a crow's nest and some common lapwings which are green on top of the body and white underneath.

Debbie

Here are some excerpts from *The Diary of a Blackbird* which was written by a fourth-year boy over a period of several weeks during the summer term. The observations result from a series of questions that he wrote down at the beginning of the period of observation: questions that he wanted answering.

May 20th Monday   12 noon
Male blackbird is singing in the ash tree to the south of the house. After about 5 minutes he flew to the scots pine in the front garden. His song is deepish and musical; he sings in bursts of song each around fifteen seconds long. First brood has left the nest.

12.15 pm
Male blackbirds down the road start to sing. The blackbird I am studying stops singing.

1.15 pm
Male blackbird feeding in garden on a few berries and worms. I have found a way to distinguish him from other blackbirds. He has a thin white streak down his back and has got a white patch on his left wing. He has also a white patch around his right eye.

May 21st Tuesday   4.15 pm
Male is singing in the ash tree; he is facing east. Every time I see him singing he is always facing east or north. I think this is because the most aggressive male blackbird is in the north or east.

May 22nd Wednesday   9.00 am
Male blackbird feeding two young ones, while the female is sitting on the nest incubating a second clutch consisting of 3 eggs. It is usually 4.

12.45 pm
Male is on the next door's roof; he has just stopped singing. Another male blackbird has flown up to him. First male flew down to the lawn. Second male followed. They fluttered into the air, clawing at each other with feet and pecking with their bills; after that they flew off in different directions.

May 25th Saturday   10 am
The male sees another female. He flies up to it and he chases her over the cornfield.

11.15 am
Male chases song thrush over cornfield for no apparent reason.

12.15 pm
Male singing on the roof; he is facing north. This is his favourite singing post probably because intruders can see him clearly and be warned.

May 27th Monday
Male has been in two fights. He has suffered feather loss. He's got a bald patch on his back but is still singing strongly. The fights were on the east borders of his territory.

May 28th Tuesday   10 am
The male has had another fight in the paddock. The other Male blackbird flew off after about 2 minutes.

12.15 pm
Male singing on the roof. The female is incubating the second clutch. This is unusual because the young blackbirds are fed by both parents, then when they leave them, then the female starts to lay another clutch.

May 29th Wednesday   9 am
Male seen with beakful of worms feeds them to the female who is incubating the second clutch of eggs. The male is singing strongly in the mornings around 8 to 9 a.m. and at dinnertime around 11.30 to 1.30. He is also singing late in the evening around 9 p.m.

May 30th Thursday
First brood are still around the male's territory I have only seen 3 when there should be 5. 8.30 pm. Still feeding them. Female is off the nest and has a fight with a male blackbird. She did not look as though she had suffered any wounds. It was in the paddock.

May 31st Friday
One of the first brood has been killed by a cat only 4 left. Female is still incubating the second clutch.

Tim

Now *you* try observing a creature. It could be a wild animal or bird or fish or insect; or a domestic animal, like a cat, dog or budgie; or a farm animal, like a cow, sheep or sheepdog.

Don't worry about the shape of what you are writing at this stage. Just concentrate on what you are looking at, smelling, touching, and hearing. Try to capture, in the details you note down, the spirit of the creature you are observing.

Our cat...

is curled up on the cushion —
can hardly tell his head from his tail —
asleep

When I get close he opens two green eyes
with black slits for pupils —
as if to say "Go back to sleep" —
he stretches his front legs out
and arches his back

Then he comes and butts me softly
on the face, purring.
He smells of sleep.

He shakes his head and it makes the
name tag on his collar jingle.
He licks his front paws and
then goes for a stroll —
over to the window where he sits
neatly tucking in his tail.
He scratches his left ear
like a bored student
and settles down to sleep
again

The blue tit

The common garden acrobat appears.
Bouncing as he flies, he flies to a tree
then the basket of nuts.
With his yellow bright breast and blue-green back
he shows off to a dull female house-sparrow,
then he flies to the bird-box,
and hops inside.
He keeps putting his head out with its black eye stripe.
Then he flies to the basket of nuts,
and hangs upside down.
Then he flies away when the starlings swoop down.

Gary Wilson

Honey the wonderdog

Lying by the warm radiator
fixing her eyes on the ball
wagging her tail
she yawns, whines
and starts washing herself.
Then puts head down
trotting into the lounge.
Sits by mum with head on her slippers
ears back
sniffs
yawns and lays down again.
Looks bored
closing eyes
looking sleepy
listens, stretches.
Then prancing over to me
licks me all over
one ear up listening
she goes over to the fire
lays down on her back.
Gets up when she hears dad coming in
runs to the door, wagging her tail
jumps up, licks, gets excited
races upstairs she collapses,
wagging.

Tracy Sleet

Christopher Smart considers his cat, Jeoffry

For I will consider my Cat Jeoffry.

For he is the servant of the Living God, duly and daily serving him.

For at the first glance of the glory of God in the East he worships in his way.

For is this done by wreathing his body seven times round with elegant quickness.

For then he leaps up to catch the musk, which is the blessing of God upon his prayer.

For he rolls upon prank to work it in.

For having done duty and received blessing he begins to consider himself.

For this he performs in ten degrees.

For first he looks upon his fore-paws to see if they are clean.

For secondly he kicks up behind to clear away there.

For thirdly he works it upon stretch with the fore-paws extended.

For fourthly he sharpens his paws by wood.

For fifthly he washes himself.

For sixthly he rolls upon wash.

For seventhly he fleas himself, that he may not be interrupted upon the beat.

For eighthly he rubs himself against a post.

For ninthly he looks up for his instructions.

For tenthly he goes in quest of food.

For having consider'd God and himself he will consider his neighbour.

For if he meets another cat he will kiss her in kindness.

For when he takes his prey he plays with it to give it chance.

For one mouse in seven escapes by his dallying.

For when his day's work is done his business more properly begins.

For he keeps the Lord's watch in the night against the adversary.

For he counteracts the powers of darkness by his electrical skin & glaring eyes.

For he counteracts the Devil, who is death, by brisking about the life.

prayers For in his morning orisons he loves the sun and the sun loves him.

For he is of the tribe of Tiger.

For the Cherub Cat is a term of the Angel Tiger.

For he has the subtlety and hissing of a serpent, which in goodness he suppresses.

For he will not do destruction, if he is well-fed, neither will he spit without provocation.

For he purrs in thankfulness, when God tells him he's a good Cat.

For he can fetch and carry, which is patience in employment.

For he can jump over a stick, which is patience upon proof positive.

For he can spraggle upon waggle at the word of command.

For he can jump from an eminence into his master's bosom.

For he can catch the cork and toss it again.

For he is hated by the hypocrite and miser.

For the former is affraid of detection.

For the latter refuses the charge.

For he camels his back to bear the first notion of business.

For he is good to think on, if a man would express himself neatly.

For he made a great figure in Egypt for his signal services.

Egyptian rat that eats crocodiles' eggs

For he killed the Ichneumon-rat very pernicious by land.
For his ears are so acute that they sting again.
For from this proceeds the passing quickness of his attention.
For by stroking of him I have found out electricity.
For, tho he cannot fly, he is an excellent clamberer.
For his motions upon the face of the earth are more than any other
  quadrupede.
For he can tread to all the measures upon the musick.
For he can swim for life.
For he can creep.

Christopher Smart

The following poem is *imagined* observation; that is to say, it wasn't directly observed at the time of writing, but was recalled to the imagination of the writer by memory. In this particular poem, the writer is working from what he saw in a book, not from actual observation. A television documentary on animals would be a good source for this kind of writing.

Living cloud

Creeping through the Amazon forest,
Vines and undergrowth part before his mighty head.
Looking like a stormcloud in the jungle.
Water glints in the moonlight.
He has come to the greatest river on earth.
He dares not cross it because of cannibal fish known as
piranhas.
His glossy shoulders go up and down like pistons.
Gracefully he leaps onto a low branch of a breadfruit tree,
Waiting for some unlucky creature to wander below the tree
that conceals him.
His four black feet brandishing claws, gripping the branch.
Suddenly the blunder buss of the Amazon forest comes.
He announces himself with a squealing whistle.
The panther's muscles tense.
Then he leaps upon the unsuspecting tapir.
Roaring he pounces on the tapir,
claws ripping, jaws biting.
The tapir gives one last squeal.
The panther drags the carcase to the river where he can
drink with his meal.

Stephen Bell

Observing people

Observing people is more difficult. You have got to be even more invisible.

Sometimes you can sit in a room and watch someone without their knowing you are looking at them. Sitting at a window looking on to the street is one way of doing this.

At other times, that may not be possible, so you will have to develop what the poet Edwin Morgan calls a 'quick, unstudied, unprying way of looking at people and things', and your memory will have to retain the many little photographs you are taking with your eyes. 'It's like using a very good silent automatic camera disguised as a pair of eyes.'

This man was seen for about thirty seconds, passing a window on the street:

His grey hair – blowing over his eyes –
untidy – he stops to read the evening paper
while his dog pees in the gutter

He's moving along slowly now
– shuffling.
His alsatian is anxious to move on.

Suddenly he comes to and sets off
at a faster than usual pace

When he looks up I can see that his
eyes are double-crossed.
His skin is heavily lined, like a prune.
He has bad teeth; grey stubble on
his chin and neck

The dog looks ill-kept: big, powerful
and vicious.
The man is wearing an old coat –
ex-army – and slippers!

What can I do with these notes? I can either leave them in my notebook as they are, or I could work on them further and try to capture *exactly* what I felt about that man.

I realize that I didn't feel anything about him as I started to make the notes, but that by the end I am making a comparison between him and the dog.

I also want to try and get down in words how this particular man is different from any other:

94

His grey hair –blowing over his eyes– ~~uncut~~ *uncut*

~~untidy~~ – he stops to read The Evening ~~paper~~ *Press*

while his ~~dog~~ pees in the gutter.
          alsatian

~~He's moving along slowly now~~   He's shuffling along now *still reading*
~~& shuffling~~   on the end of the
                                        dog's lead
~~this alsatian is anxious to move on.~~

                    he's yanked forward
Suddenly ~~he comes to and sets off~~

~~at a faster than usual pace~~

   and pulled along towards a lamppost

so he pulls hard on the lead

which tightens round the dog's neck

   and the dog stops.

Now
~~when he looks up~~ I can see ~~that~~ his

~~eyes are~~ double –crossed eyes,
                              wrinkles
His ~~skin is~~ (heavily lined), /like a prune

He has bad teeth; grey stubble on

   his chin and neck.

            ~~it kept. big powerful vicious~~
The dog is smouldering, resentful.

He hits it. It snarls back.

Then follows after his tired slippers.

~~The man is wearing an old coat –~~
~~ex-army & and slippers.~~

What changes have I made? Are they the changes I said I would make, or is the poem taking on a life of its own and making its own decisions?

One thing that is clear now is that the observations are grouping themselves into sections of three lines each:

His grey uncut hair blowing over his eyes
he stops to read The Evening Press
while his alsatian pees in the gutter.

He's shuffling along now, still reading,
on the end of the dog's lead.
Suddenly he's yanked forward towards a lamp-post.

So he pulls hard on the lead
which tightens round the dog's neck
and the dog stops dead.

Now I can see his double-crossed eyes,
his heavily-lined skin wrinkling like a prune;
his bad teeth, his unshaven chin.

The dog is angry, resentful.
He hits it. It snarls back,
then follows after his tired slippers.

Looking at people

When I've got nothing to do –
like waiting at a bus-stop
or standing in a bank-queue –
I look at people.

I look at them going along in a car,
but imagine the car isn't there,
so that they seem to be speeding along in mid-air
at 40 mph in a relaxed sitting position,
talking to each other and laughing as though this was nothing,
and the driver juggling with the air,
his hair as still as in the adverts.
It's incredible!
Even better if a cyclist goes by:
he looks as if he's treading air,
sitting up like a bear
but about a foot off the ground;
or on a racer, with legs going like pistons,
and leaning forward ridiculously
with his bum in the air.
Or imagine a bus conductress
swinging on the back of an invisible bus
like the happiest person in the world,
not looking where she is going . . .

Observing places

The following poem was written by Danny Marriott, a pupil in a school in London. He was looking at an old warehouse in a deserted dock:

The old warehouse

The windows are smashed,
They are making shapes with the cracks.
The wind bellows through the rubble.
The pigeons are cooing as they sit on the bricks.
The feathers on their wings
Clatter away as I take one step.
The scruffy buildings are not in use,
So the pigeons have made an empire of their own,
Where the ruler sits in fear of humans
Marching through like the Romans on their
RAMPAGE!

You too can write about the buildings and places around your school – either during a special lesson in which your teacher takes you out with a notebook, or on your way home, for homework. By selecting details from what he saw, Danny has given us a clear idea of how he *feels* about the warehouse; and yet all he has done is describe what he saw.

When Danny got back to school, he read a bit about the history of the old warehouse, looked at some pictures of what it was like when it was in use, listened to stories from his parents and grandparents about it, and imagined what it would have been like to *work* there.

Then he wrote this poem, taking the voice of someone trying to get work at the warehouse:

Chainman

As the hinges start to creak
We push and push to turn the chain,
Just waiting to hear our name.
The ganger's in sight so they start to fight,
Only to work through the day.
My hat comes off as the man
Behind me raises his hand just to be called out.
The gangers go by,
My stomach is hurting as I'm pushing on the chain,
Just waiting to be called out.
I'm not called out.
I walk away while the beggar
Shouts 'My name is! My name is! My name is!'

The following poem was written as a piece of homework. I was asked by my English teacher to write a poem entitled 'On the South Side of the Thames'. I later changed this title to 'South Side'. This meant I had a chance to put down on paper all the little things I have noticed walking through the streets of south London. I must say though, that in this poem I have only put down the bad things about south London. There are a lot of good things I can think about it. I might even go on to write a poem including the good things about south London. I will have to see whether I get round to it.

South side

Newspapers and crisp packets
Drunk men with dirty jackets
Old cars with tyres stripped
Rubbish heaps where junk's been tipped
On the South side of the Thames.

Dirty faces, wearing rags
Used matches and ends of fags
Smoke and dirt from old cars
Smashed bottles and cracked jars
On the South side of the Thames.

Old tunnels full of dirt
Old people watching, feelings hurt
Grey walls full of graffiti
Big kids strong and meaty
On the South side of the Thames.

Broken street-lamp lights the night
Two youths quarrel and have a fight
Rag and bone men on horses and carts
Smoke in the pubs and the sound of darts
On the South side of the Thames.

Brown leaves, shrivelled flowers in a window box
Old ladies with nylon coats, wishing they were fox
Terraced houses pushing out smoke
Kids drinking water, wishing it was Coke
On the South side of the Thames.

James Smith

There is no substitute for actually going out and looking at a place before you write. Much writing is about experience – direct, actual experience – and it was the experience of a visit to a local factory that inspired the following poems:

Factory dream

As a child I loved sweets and,
Sat dreaming of working in a
   sweet factory –
Mmm polos, crunchy kit kat,
   colourful smarties,
Eating all day long.
The dream shatters,
Imagination becomes reality.
Clock on at seven, change into
   overalls, don paper hats.
Stare bleary-eyed at people
   clocking off.
I jump out of the way of the
   miniature tractors, taking boxed
   goodies for loading onto
   shop lorries.
Passing reservoirs of chocolate,
   being poured into the smartie
   moulds.
I climb onto a vacant stool,
   pushing lids onto smartie tubes,
   watching them disappear along
   endless conveyor belts.
My sleepy eyes gaze at the swing
   doors to see a group of children appear.
Good grief, don't we ever get a
   rest from stupid questions?
     they ask.
They disappear round a corner,
   and I gaze down at the
     never-ending tubes.
Seeing sweets all day. Who eats
   them all.
I wish I'd never seen a sweet.
How I wish I was back at school.

Samantha Sweeney

Boredom

Blick
My day has started
I walk and walk
along the never ending
   corridors
Left and right turns
Here and there
Up some stairs
And through a door
The noise hits me
Like a bang on the head
I nod to my friends
And they smile back
No use talking, you see
I walk quickly to my place
And sit down on the chair
Still warm from the last shift
I begin my same old job
Filling up Smartie tubes
The ones the machine has missed
For several hours I sit here
Then someone taps me on the
   shoulder
He points to the clock on
   the wall
Time to go
Doors, corridors, stairs
Again
The end of another day
Blick

Rachel Allen

About writing poems 2

Drafts of a poem written on a school trip

On a school trip to Oxford, the teacher asked his students to make notes about things they saw that interested them, so that they could later write them up into poems. Here are three drafts made by one of the students, Katy Robson:

NEW COLLEGE
old blended with new - new unsightly
strange smell - like air freshener
carpet on the floor - small intricate design in red and blue
wood and stone - carved archways in wood rather than stone
large portraits of various men - richly dressed in bright clothes -
blues, purples, reds, golds and greens
wooden ceiling - carved
wall filled with statues - Jesus in the middle nailed to the cross
At the top God - hand raised as if in blessing - flanked by angels. Each
face different - holding various objects - pipes, swords, staff
lighter chapel than the other

STATUE: grotesque - swathed in bandages like a living mummy
Eyes open wide - staring into space
large unnatural hands - long fingers - somehow out of
proportion - broken neck - at an unnatural angle and pose

ABOVE STATUE - stained glass window - pictures seem to be painted
on, rather than individual pieces of glass. Picture continuous
rather than individual pictures

SECOND DRAFT

Grotesque, with distorted shape.
Swathed in bandages like a living mummy.
Eyes open wide staring into emptiness.
Large unnatural hands with stretched-out fingers
stands   He ~~stood~~ stiffly upright,
With neck bent backwards – twisted as if in disgrace.
No expression of pain on his face,
is   Yet his pose ~~was~~ uncomfortable – unnatural.

falls   Soft light ~~fell~~ on the statue from above.
Sunlight seeping through the coloured windows,
Deep warm colours.

THIRD DRAFT

Lazarus

Grotesque, with distorted shape.
Swathed in bandages like a living mummy.
Eyes open wide – staring, his face expressionless.
Large unnatural hands with outstretched fingers.
He stands stiffly upright
With neck bent backwards – twisted
As if in disgrace.
No sign of pain on his face
Yet his pose is uncomfortable.

Sunlight seeps through the painted windows from above
And falls on the cold, grey statue
Bringing warmth to his lonely vigil.

This is a transcript of a conversation Katy had with her teacher about the writing of the poem:

T. How does the finished poem compare to your first draft?

K. First of all what I did was just make notes: words and phrases about everything I saw. The statue bit was what I wrote least about, but I got a poem out of it, whereas the rest of what I wrote was rubbish really.

T. Why did you get a poem out of that bit and not the rest?

K. I don't know . . . the rest was just description, whereas this seemed more personal.

T. If that piece on Lazarus wasn't description, then what was it?

K. The others were pure description, like 'grey stones', the sun shining and so on; whereas this was more describing the expression on his face, and the way he looked to me rather than the way he looked to everybody.

T. So when did you actually write the first draft: on location, as it were, or later on, when you came back home?

K. I did that when I came back.

T. What about the 'shape' of the poem? How did that evolve? Did it come out like that first time?

K. The second draft was split into two, yes; but the first time it was all jumbled up together.

T. Why is there a split there?

K. When you saw the statue, there were windows above and you could just see the light falling. It wasn't actually about the statue, it was about the windows and the sunlight – sort of separate from it.

T. What do you feel now about the third draft?

K. It's OK.

T. Do you think you could go further with it – or do you think you've 'arrived' at what you wanted to say?

K. I think it's as far as I'll get, but it's still not quite right, if you see what I mean.

T. What's not right about it?

K. I don't really know. It's just . . . it sounds as if it's too horrible, whereas it wasn't really . . .

Here is Katy's final draft:

Lazarus

Alone – separated from his friends
The lonely statue stands and stares.
He exists in our world.
He had no choice, but was created
By a sculptor's feverish hand;
Thrust into a cold uncaring world,
He waits patiently for his fate.
Death holds no fear for him,
He has died before.
Yet he is resurrected in a block of stone
To show the power of man's faith.

Subject matter

Poems, as it was said at the beginning of this book, can be about *anything*. In fact, they can be about the most ordinary of experiences, like getting up, having breakfast, and going out:

I am glad to be up and about

I am glad to be up and about this sunny morning,
Walking the raised path between fields,
While all around me
Are cheerful folk harvesting potatoes.

I am glad to be away from books,
Broadcasts and the familiar smells,
And the unending pursuit of a livelihood.

Small boys on their way to school
Trail their toes through the stripped soil,
And pounce with joy
Upon the marble-size potatoes left behind by the harvesters,
And with these fill their satchels.

One voice is raised in song,
While the men, hunkering on their heels,
Move up in a line like pirates
To uncover the heaps of buried treasure,
And transfer them to baskets.

And girls who should be playing with dolls
Unload the baskets into sacks
Which tonight or tomorrow night
Will be speeding in a groaning truck
To Karachi, a thousand miles away.

And this week or the following week,
Bilious businessmen and irate wives
And their washed and prattling children,
Will sit down at uncounted tables
And hastily devour the potatoes I see
With never a thought for these
Fields, these men and this sunny morning.

Taufiq Rafat

An un-African breakfast

(spoken to a free guitar accompaniment)

So here I am this morning
Early in the kitchen.

The aroma of fresh coffee on the boil,
   Nose-filling aroma of good fresh coffee
     on the boil;
   And this kitchen is good to be in
   And good to hear the browning water
     babble-bubbling inside the glass-trap
     head of the percolator;
And the good wife still asleep in her vono bed
Dreaming good dreams, I hope,
Of me!

All night the tummy hasn't been well,
   Running like it wanted nothing more
     to do with me for eating what I
     do not know –
   All night a running tummy;
   Till at last out of weariness
I drop into oblivion between 4 and 5
   Quite unknowing –
     Deep oblivion
     Sweet as feathers . . .

Then crash out of nowhere
The white day comes bursting in
   Through frosted louvres . . .

And it's good to be alive!

Good indeed to be alive,
   So thank we god
   For everything,
     And the myriad sparrows
     Chirruping in the fresh morning sun outside
     While the percolator bubbles.

And here a loaf of bread
And there a jar of marmalade
And sugar for the dreaming wife
And milk just turned out of its blue tin
   now rolling
   on its back
   like a cat,
And there the frying-pan on the gas cooker
   And two eggs spluttering away –
     Yolk of golden egg with garnishing of
      onion and new-cut pepper green and
      winking red,
And a little salt
   A little salt . . .

Oh damn!
A hot speck of spitting oil near got me
In the eye.

Yes reader
What d'you say?

Oh, mustn't I?
    Mustn't drink good coffee in the
        morning,
    Mustn't eat good bread and marmalade
        for breakfast,
    Mustn't fry eggs over a gas cooker
        While my good wife
        Still lies dreaming,
And mustn't read books, I suppose,
Nor write poetry,
    Because –
What d'you say?
    Because
    Not African!

But listen
The radio in my sitting room
(I should have told you of the radio):
Listen –
    Drum sounds on *15 megacycles*
    signalling the new day in Africa,
    Pop sounds
    Calling the waking continent
    To the Breakfast Show,
    Many-tongued voices
Daring all men everywhere
    To breathe in the dawn-fresh winds
    Blowing across a changing world.

And the warrior chieftains pass on
And the beaded maidens dance away
And we sit by the running waters
    And sigh for an innocence that is gone.

But here –
    The eggs are done;

And still it's good to be alive!

And though I cannot whistle out loud
I know there is joy
    Bubbling like coffee inside me,
Sweet aromatic joy
    Of being alive,
    So thank we god
        For everything
        And the myriad sparrows
        Chirruping in the fresh morning sun outside
        While the percolator babbles,
And I feel coming alive within me
The first movement of an un-African poem.

Joe de Graft

Lyrics

Definition of the word 'lyric': originally a poem or recitation meant to be sung to the accompaniment of the lyre (a small harp), but now attributed to any short poem in stanzas expressing personal feeling.

The clearest connection between this definition and music today is in the 'lyrics' of songs. Many singers and groups print the lyrics of their songs on the record cover. Sometimes the lyrics are printed in book form, or in sheet music.

When you have collected as many lyrics together as you can, and have them in front of you in the classroom, read them aloud and then ask yourself the following questions:

If you already know how they sound when sung, what is your reaction?

If you haven't heard the song, do you think the lyrics stand by themselves as poetry? What do you think of the 'treatment' of the lyrics when sung? Does the experience of listening to the song change your attitude toward the printed lyrics?

Who would you say were the really good lyric writers (i) at the moment (ii) in the last thirty years?

What comes first, the lyrics or the music (i) in the composing of a song (ii) to you personally, when you listen to a song?

Do all the lyrics that you have in front of you have anything in common? Think about subject-matter, form, rhyming and other features of poetry that you have come across in this book.

It is always possible to write to record companies and ask them to send you spare record covers with lyrics on them, explaining that you need them for a wall display or project.

'She dwelt among the untrodden ways'

She dwelt among the untrodden ways
    Beside the springs of Dove,
A Maid whom there were none to praise
    And very few to love:

A violet by a mossy stone
    Half hidden from the eye!
– Fair as a star, when only one
    Is shining in the sky.

She lived unknown, and few could know
    When Lucy ceased to be;
But she is in her grave, and, oh,
    The difference to me!

William Wordsworth

A *supernova* is an enormous stellar explosion in a nebula, or cluster of gases, which leaves a dense residue of rock, known as a 'white dwarf'. A book on the formation of stars and planets was the inspiration for this song by Dave Harland:

Orion nebula

Time's running out, it's time to escape
from Orion Nebula, before it's too late
Star's going crazy, going to explode
one last thrust of Orion's sword.

The star's getting hotter, swelling so fast
polar caps melting, life just can't last
Burnt to a cinder, world ends in fire
the White Dwarf is coming . . . Supernova.

We left in search of a solar system
looking for a planet we can live on
Light years away signals were heard
Could it be life? That's surely absurd.

Uranus and Neptune, colder than ice
Pluto is black, blacker than night
Travelling on, towards the sunlight
Saturnian rings, glistening white.

Jupiter giant fills up the sky
Mars the red planet, but there's no life
Bright in the morning, brighter at night
Venus is beckoning, shimmering light.

Planet Earth, the signal is strong
Journey is ending, nightmare is gone
Life-giving planet, carpet of green
Orion Nebula, now a bad dream.

Dave says of his song:

I became interested in stars and star-formation while at school. I decided I wanted to write a song about this subject so I looked for books that would tell me more. It was the sound of the words 'Supernova', 'White and Red Dwarves' and 'Nebula' that caught my imagination. This was the most important thing to me in the composition of the song: finding the subject-matter and the sound of the key words. I suppose I got the tune in my head before I found the words. I looked for words that would rhyme and create a pattern within which I could write. Then I filled in the rest.

Each verse has the same basic musical pattern:

Speeches

A good speech not only has to communicate a message, it has to communicate it well. The best speech-makers know that when they are addressing a large crowd, they must make their message simple, clear and well-phrased. There must be a rhythm and structure to their words. Such features of rhythm and structure as repetition, pausing, timing and emphasis are shared with poetry, especially poetry that is public and declamatory rather than private and meditative: the kind of poetry that needs to be read to crowds over a megaphone or microphone.

This connection between speech-making (oratory) and poetry can be made clearer if we look at this extract from one of Jimmy Reid's addresses. Jimmy Reid is a Clydeside union man, and a powerful speaker on issues affecting working people everywhere. Here, he is talking about alienation in society:

> Many may not have rationalized it. May not even understand, may not be able to articulate it. But they feel it. It therefore conditions and colours their social attitudes. Alienation expresses itself in different ways among different people. It is to be found in what our courts often describe as 'the criminal anti-social behaviour of a section of the community'. It is expressed by those young people who want to opt out of society, by drop outs, the so-called maladjusted, those who seek to escape permanently from the reality of society through intoxicants and narcotics.

If we set this out as poetry, line by line, according to the rhythmic phrasing of the speech, the connection is obvious:

> Many may not have rationalized it.
> May not even understand,
> may not be able to understand it.
> But they feel it . . .

The size of the audience is a crucial factor in deciding what kind of voice to adopt. A small group will probably require a quieter voice, and be able to accept a more complicated, personal style; a crowd needs a more direct message – which is why some Russian poets, who read to large crowds regularly, have developed a more outward-going style of poetry.

Speeches and poetry of this kind have a clear purpose: to change people's minds.

Here is an example of a poem that uses the patterns and rhythms of speech-making:

> I'm talking about the waste
> I'm talking about the waste of talent
> of time
> of money
> of effort
> It's unemployment I'm talking about.
> Had you guessed?
> Yes, not having a job,
> sitting on your backside all day
> wishing yourself away
> draining yourself away
> with no satisfaction, no pay –
> It isn't funny!

I'm talking about boredom
I'm talking about hours in front of a telly
I'm talking about pride

I am talking about the ruin of my life
I am talking about the strain on me and the wife

I am talking about my own integrity
and I don't think you're listening.

    Unlike most printed poetry, this has the feel of speaking directly to an audience. It has some of the qualities of conversation, but is one-way.

You say you care
You say you are doing things for the people
    that you were elected by the people
    and that you will act for the people

I don't believe it!
Our faith has been disappointed
We are ready for change
and we will fight for change

And you, and your armies,
your rules, your banks, your factories:
you had better watch out!
You had better look out of your windows now,
    before it's too late!

Poetry of the instant

'From the beginning it is obvious that the poetry of the instant present cannot have the same body or the same motion as the poetry of the before and after. It can never submit to the same conditions. It is never finished. There is no rhythm which returns upon itself, no serpent of eternity with its tail in its own mouth. There is no static perfection, none of that finality which we find so satisfying because we are so frightened.

Much has been written about free verse. But all that can be said, first and last, is that free verse is, or should be, direct utterance from the instant, whole man. It is the soul and mind and body surging at once, nothing left out. They all speak together. There is some confusion, some discord. But the confusion and the discord only belong to the reality, as noise belongs to the plunge of water. It is no use inventing fancy laws for free verse, no use drawing a melodic line which all the feet must toe. Free verse toes no melodic line, no matter what the drill sergeant. Whitman pruned away his clichés – perhaps his clichés of rhythm as well of phrase. And that is about all we can do, deliberately, with free verse. We can get rid of the stereotyped movements and the old hackneyed associations of sound and sense. We can break down those artificial conduits and canals through which we do so love to force our utterance. We can break the stiff neck of habit. We can be in ourselves spontaneous and flexible as flame, we can see that utterance rushes out without artificial form or artificial sweetness. But we cannot positively prescribe any motion, any rhythm. All the laws we invent or discover – it amounts to pretty much the same – will fail to apply to free verse. They will only apply to some form of restricted un-free verse.'

D. H. Lawrence: INTRODUCTION TO AMERICAN EDITION OF NEW POEMS

Kangaroo

In the northern hemisphere
Life seems to leap at the air, or skim under the wind
Like stags on rocky ground, or pawing horses, or springy scut-tailed rabbits.
Or else rush horizontal to charge at the sky's horizon,
Like bulls or bisons or wild pigs.

Or slip like water slippery towards its ends,
As foxes, stoats, and wolves, and prairie dogs.

Only mice, and moles, and rats, and badgers, and beavers, and perhaps bears
Seem belly-plumbed to the earth's mid-navel.
Or frogs that when they leap come flop, and flop to the centre of the earth.

But the yellow antipodal Kangaroo, when she sits up,
Who can unseat her, like a liquid drop that is heavy, and just touches earth.

The downward drip
The down-urge.
So much denser than cold-blooded frogs.

Delicate mother Kangaroo
Sitting up there rabbit-wise, but huge, plumb-weighted,
And lifting her beautiful slender face, oh! so much more
     gently and finely lined than a rabbit's, or than a hare's,
Lifting her face to nibble at a round white peppermint
     drop, which she loves, sensitive mother Kangaroo.

Her sensitive, long, pure-bred face.
Her full antipodal eyes, so dark,
So big and quiet and remote, having watched so many empty dawns in silent Australia.

Her little loose hands, and drooping Victorian shoulders.
And then her great weight below the waist, her vast pale belly
With a thin young yellow little paw hanging out, and
     straggle of a long thin ear, like a ribbon,
Like a funny trimming to the middle of her belly, thin
     little dangle of an immature paw, and one thin ear.

Her belly, her big haunches
And, in addition, the great muscular python-stretch of her tail.

There, she shan't have any more peppermint drops.
So she wistfully, sensitively sniffs the air, and then turns, goes off in slow sad leaps

On the long flat skis of her legs,
Steered and propelled by that steel-strong snake of a tail.

Stops again, half turns, inquisitive to look back.
While something stirs quickly in her belly, and a lean
     little face comes out, as from a window,

Peaked and a bit dismayed,
Only to disappear again quickly away from the sight of
     the world, to snuggle down in the warmth,
Leaving the trail of a different paw hanging out.

Still she watches with eternal, cocked wistfulness!
How full her eyes are, like the full, fathomless, shining eyes of an Australian black-boy
Who has been lost so many centuries on the margins of existence!

She watches with insatiable wistfulness.
Untold centuries of watching for something to come,
For a new signal from life, in that silent lost land of the South.

Where nothing bites but insects and snakes and the sun, small life.
Where no bull roared, no cow ever lowed, no stag cried,
     No leopard screeched, no lion coughed, no dog barked,
But all was silent save for parrots occasionally, in the haunted blue bush.

Wistfully watching, with wonderful liquid eyes.
And all her weight, all her blood, dripping sack-wise down towards the earth's centre,
And the live little-one taking in its paw at the door of her belly.

Leap then, and come down on the line that draws to the earth's deep, heavy centre.

D. H. Lawrence

Answers and parodies

When Christopher Marlowe published the following love poem in 1599, Sir Walter Ralegh answered him the next year with a poem in the same style and same form, but with a different message:

The passionate shepherd to his love

Come live with me and be my love,
And we will all the pleasures prove,
That hills and valleys, dales and fields,
And all the craggy mountains yields.

There we will sit upon the rocks,
And see the shepherds feed their flocks,
By shallow rivers to whose falls
Melodious birds sing madrigals.

And I will make thee beds of roses
With a thousand fragrant posies,
A cap of flowers, and a kirtle
Embroidered all with leaves of myrtle;

A gown made of the finest wool
Which from our pretty lambs we pull;
Fair lined slippers for the cold,
With buckles of the purest gold;

A belt of straw and ivy buds,
With coral clasps and amber studs:
And if these pleasures may thee move,
Come live with me and be my love.

The shepherd's swains shall dance and sing
For thy delight each May morning:
If these delights thy mind may move,
Then live with me and be my love.

Christopher Marlowe

Answer to Marlowe

If all the world and love were young,
And truth in every shepherd's tongue,
These pretty pleasures might me move
To live with thee and be thy love.

Time drives the flocks from field to fold,
When rivers rage and rocks grow cold,
And Philomel becometh dumb;
The rest complain of cares to come.

The flowers do fade, and wanton fields
To wayward winter reckoning yields;
A honey tongue, a heart of gall,
Is fancy's spring, but sorrow's fall.

Thy gowns, thy shoes, thy beds of roses,
Thy cap, thy kirtle, and thy posies
Soon break, soon wither, soon forgotten,
In folly ripe, in reason rotten.

Thy belt of straw and ivy buds,
Thy coral clasps and amber studs,
All these in me no means can move
To come to thee and be thy love.

But could youth last and love still breed,
Had joys no date nor age no need,
Then these delights my mind might move
To live with thee and be thy love.

Sir Walter Ralegh

Nearly four hundred years later, two pupils from a school in Northampton wrote parodies of the Marlowe poem, setting their poems in the modern world:

Come live with me

Come live with me and be my love
And we will all the pleasures
  prove.
Provided you can pay your way
'Cos I need your money if you
  want to stay.

We can sit upon a number nine
  bus
And gaze at each other with
  desire and lust
As we pass the gas works and
  the park
And the sun descends and the bus
  goes dark.

And in the morning when we
  finally awake
And wonder why we shiver and
  shake,
We realise that they've done it
  at last
And cut off the electricity and
  the gas.

And when at last the summer doth
  come
You can sit in the noon-day sun
And read of dresses you can't
  afford.
And pictures of things you'd
  like to own.

I hope these words do not spoil
  my offer
To come and live with me . . .
  in squalor.

Robert Wright

Come live with me and be my love

Come live with me and be my love!
Not in a mansion but the flat
  above.
It's not very big, but grand
  enough
For you and me and all our
  stuff.

Love is free as it ought to be
Though the mortgage is high at
  No. 3
We'll live on love and not a lot
But we'll get by with what
  we've got.

We'll have to get some curtains
  though
For our caressing is on show.
Windows are bereft of curtains
  and paint
And love may be blind but the
  neighbours ain't.

Lisa Salsbury

How would you 'answer' or parody the following poems?

The tyger

Tyger! Tyger! burning bright
In the forests of the night,
What immortal hand or eye
Could frame thy fearful symmetry?

In what distant deeps or skies
Burnt the fire of thine eyes?
On what wings dare he aspire?
What the hand dare seize the fire?

And what shoulder, & what art,
Could twist the sinews of thy heart?
And when thy heart began to beat,
What dread hand? & what dread feet?

What the hammer? what the chain?
In what furnace was thy brain?
What the anvil? what dread grasp
Dare its deadly terrors clasp?

When the stars threw down their spears
And water'd heaven with their tears,
Did he smile his work to see?
Did he who made the Lamb make thee?

Tyger! Tyger! burning bright
In the forests of the night,
What immortal hand or eye
Dare frame they fearful symmetry?

William Blake

Lines written in early spring

I heard a thousand blended notes,
While in a grove I sate reclined,
In that sweet mood when pleasant thoughts
Bring sad thoughts to the mind.

To her fair works did nature link
The human soul that through me ran;
And much it grieved my heart to think
What man has made of man.

Through primrose tufts, in that green bower,
The periwinkle trailed its wreaths;
And 'tis my faith that every flower
Enjoys the air it breathes.

The birds around me hopped and played;
Their thoughts I cannot measure:
But the least motion which they made,
It seemed a thrill of pleasure.

The budding twigs spread our their fan,
To catch the breezy air;
And I must think, do all I can,
That there was pleasure there.

If this belief from heaven be sent,
If such be Nature's holy plan,
Have I not reason to lament
What man has made of man?

William Wordsworth

Working from newspapers

Features, headlines, articles and stories in newspapers can provide the raw material that can be fashioned into a poem. Often, such material is unwittingly 'poetic' in urgency of feeling, its expression or its theme.

It was while reading a short article in a daily newspaper that I felt urged to write the following poems. The irony of the situation in which a woman with an unwanted pregnancy meets a woman who wants, but cannot for medical reasons have a child, struck me very strongly . . .

Unspoken thoughts at the family planning clinic

I

I am not here because I'm ill,
I'm here because I want something.
I want what you've got:
a baby growing in your belly.

I have a man who is warm and loving.
We love with tenderness and passion
in the dark infertile afternoon
in the dark unfecund night.

I hate the sterility of this clinic.
I hate the sterility of town,
the blank pages of the magazines
with their empty, fruitless dreams.

My body is crying out for a baby.
Can you hear me on your side of the waiting room?
I am ready, I want it now.
I am not bitter, but I am unhappy.

II

Yes, I hear you. Don't worry.
On your side of the room
you have nothing to worry about.
I've got a child I don't want in my womb.

Oh I know the father, yes.
Don't think bad of me, will you?
I knew and loved him, he loved me,
but now we're through.

I'm doing this for love, can you believe me?
It has come too soon, I'm not ready.
I need someone who will stay with me
who wants more than just going steady.

I'd like to give this baby to you
before it becomes a part of me.
I'd like to give this to you
to make you happy.

115

The following newspaper article can be used as source material for a poem setting the story of the Garden of Eden in the present.

Visit to the Garden of Eden ends with an apple fall

David Blundy

And He placed at the east of the Garden of Eden cherubims and a flaming sword (Genesis iii, 24).

IF Adam and Eve walked east of the Garden of Eden today, as I did last week, they would find the view distinctly more prosaic. They would cross a little bridge over the River Jordan and run up against the high, steel security fence and watchtowers of the Kibbutz Bet Zera, erected as protection not from the Serpent of Genesis but a more recent enemy, the Palestinian Liberation Organisation.

They would then hit the road from Tiberius to Bet Shean and dodge between the trailers taking tanks and armoured personnel carriers to the Lebanese front. Above they would hear the gentle rumble of Israeli fighter-bombers patrolling the Syrian forces in the Bekaa valley, and a mile or two in front lies the electrified fence marking the border of Jordan and Israel. It would become clear to them that God meant it when he said: "Behold the man is become as one of us to know Good and Evil."

According to an American and a Czechoslovakian geolo-gist, the first human creatures lived more than two million years ago at a place called Ubeidiya in what is now Israel. They were unprepossessing people with thick necks and no chins. The scientists, writing in the magazine Nature, said they lived as much as 500,000 years before Africa's homo erectus.

For Israelis, stricken by the Lebanese war, it was the first piece of really good news for a long time. The newspapers made the most of it. "Garden of Eden may have been near Afikim" (a nearby kibbutz), the Jerusalem Post said on its front page.

The news does not seem to have filtered down to the present-day dwellers of para-dise. "What are you looking for?" asked an irritated man picking cotton about a mile from the spot. "The Garden of Eden? Is it a hotel?" It is, in fact, a series of trenches reminiscent of a First World War battlefield from which the crucial evidence has been dug up and sifted—a piece of human tooth, pieces of skull, stone implements and the fos-silised remains of lemmings and muskrats.

The scientists say early man would have shared the terrain with strange animals, from primitive bears to zebrine horses. Zalman Vinogradov, the founder and curator of the local Bet Gordan museum, has a vivid idea of what life was like in those days. "We are standing on the shore of a huge lake," said Vinogradov pointing towards the kibbutz swimming pool. "A bull with huge horns, the spotted hyena and a horse with five toes have come to drink.

"One day the hunters find a young hippo coming from the water. They cook it and all the people have a picnic here by the lake. After thty finished, they dig a hole and put all the bones into it. We found the bones and they have small scratches made by primitive stone tools. They liked bone marrow and you can see where they opened up the bones."

Vinogradov dismisses the Garden of Eden, the Serpent and the Tree of Knowledge as a Mesopotamic myth brought by Abraham comparatively recently, in the 18th century BC. It was perhaps no more than a coincidence that as I drove away from the area a lorry spilled its load of large, green apples.

The Sunday Times 10th October 1982

By taking the voice of:
Adam
Eve
the irritated man in the cotton field
a witness at the trial of Adam and Eve
the serpent
an archaeologist excavating the site
an Israeli fighter pilot passing overhead
– or all of these voices! – you could write a poem or poems to do justice to the article, and to explore the relationship between myth and reality, the relationship between men and women that the myth implies, the 'Fall' as seen in present-day terms, or any other theme that grips you from this story. Use the account in Genesis if you wish.

What are the possibilities for some kind of performance arising from this work?

The following poem is an answer to the question, 'How do *you* think the world began?':

The first few seconds

The world was always there.
No one put it where it is –
'I'll have it over here . . . no, there' –
No one put it there
because humans or monsters were not invented.
That is as far as man knows.

Was it blank or not?
People say Adam and Eve were the first humans invented.
And some say Apes were first to start man.
If this story is true, I don't think so:
how could humans give birth to apes
or the other way round?
Somehow it's nonsense.

There is a real true story
but as far as I know nobody will ever know it.
Maybe nothing was ever invented,
maybe we're nothing, just an imagination . . .
but that sounds a bit silly too.
Maybe God is not true.
You try asking him.

Maybe the world was attached to another planet
and had wars, so God thought
it was best to separate them.
But if you hear someone say
Adam and Eve were first on earth,
say not to me but run.

Collin Cameron

About writing poems 3

It gave me the chance of saying everything that I wanted to without being told off, because it was poetry.

My first encounter with poetry was at the local Eisteddfod. At the age of four I had to recite 'Daddy Fell Into the Pond'. I remember the weeks of preparation, trying to get each sentence in the right order. When the actual day came, I don't remember feeling nervous at all, in fact, I think I quite enjoyed everyone listening to me. I still have the certificate which says that I came joint second in the seven years and under section.

School was the next stage in my life. In the playground we would often chant rhymes as we skipped with long ropes. One of these which seems to have stuck in my memory was:

> I'm a little girl guide dressed in blue,
> These are the actions I must do.
> Salute to the Officer,
> Curtsy to the Queen
> And show my knickers to the football team.

This was never chanted if teachers were within hearing distance, since it was considered to be 'a bit rude'.

At the age of five I was taken to an elocution teacher, after telling my mum that I wanted to be a television announcer when I grew up. I was allowed to choose poetry that I liked and then read it out, trying desperately to pronounce each word correctly and remembering not to miss the 't's' off the end of words. I tended to choose poetry that was about naughty children, such as Jasper, Geranium, James and Jo who:

> . . . asked
> Their Uncles
> And Aunts
> to tea,
> And shouted
> In loud,
> Rude voices
> 'We
> Are tired
> Of scoldings
> And sendings
> To bed;
> Now
> The grown-ups
> Shall be
> Punished instead.'

It gave me the chance of saying everything that I wanted to without being told off, because it was poetry.

Eventually I graduated to poems like 'The Highwayman' by Alfred Noyes and 'Home Thoughts from Abroad' by Robert Browning.

The first poem that I ever wrote myself was called 'Firework Memories'. It was not particularly good, but it gave me a feeling of achievement. My second attempt at poetry was actually printed in the 1980 school magazine. It was not particularly good, but it filled up an awkwardly shaped space.

Poems of protest

All poetry is political in the sense that it is an act, a message between people. Even if you write poems for your eyes only, it is a political fact that you are communicating to yourself and not to others.

But some poetry is more overtly and consciously political. One example of this kind of poetry is the poetry of protest. It tends to be characterized by a straight-forwardness, a directness that is often missing in more private, less urgent writing.

Protest poems can take various forms. This one is sung by roadmenders in Balaghat, India. The first stanza is sung by men, the second by women:

The roadmenders' song

Hungry and thirsty we break these stones in the heat of the sun.
The chips of stone fly up and batter our naked bodies.
Our life is empty and useless.
Our naked bodies shine with sweat, the tears flow from our eyes.
Sometimes the chips of stone pierce the flesh, and the blood flows.
Those who have plenty of money gorge themselves with food, and live
    peacefully at home.
But it is when the heat is greatest that we have the heaviest work.
The ground burns beneath our feet: the sky blazes above.
The hot wind scorches our faces: why cannot we escape?
Sometimes the young men and girls die by the roadside,
Yet my sinful life will not leave me.

O mother, how long must I break these stones?
I am tired of living any longer.
In the cold days when all are warm in bed,
Then I must be breaking stones on the frosty ground.
In the night sleep comes not because of the cold.
All this I do and what do I get for it?
Only two annas for a long day's toil.
All this I do for my children's sake to keep them alive.
My flesh wastes away with this suffering: only my bones remain.
O that I might die quickly, and return to earth in a different form!
Hungry and thirsty we break these stones in the cold of winter.

Here are some more protest poems:

Black and white

We met
We fell
We stood together
Yet everyone said
We were not meant
for each other.
You were white
I was black.

Yet in spite
of what they said
we stood together.
They did not want that.
They tried their best
And in the end
they broke us up.

They made you
Think the worst of me
But they'll find out
One day
That you can't
always keep black
And white
Apart forever.

Colleen Mayers

119

Africa

Africa my Africa
Africa of proud warriors in ancestral savannahs
Africa of whom my grandmother sings
On the banks of the distant river
I have never known you
But your blood flows in my veins
Your beautiful black blood that irrigates the fields
The blood of your sweat
The sweat of your work
The work of your slavery
The slavery of your children
Africa tell me Africa
Is this you this back that is bent
This back that breaks under the weight of humiliation
This back trembling with red scars
And saying yes to the whip under the midday sun
But a grave voice answers me
Impetuous son that tree young and strong
That tree there
In splendid loneliness amidst white and faded flowers
That is Africa your Africa
That grows again patiently obstinately
And its fruit gradually acquire
The bitter taste of liberty.

David Diop

This poem, written by Bertolt Brecht during the rise of Nazism in Germany, is heavily sarcastic in tone:

The ballad of paragraph 218

Please, doctor. I've missed my monthly . . .
Why, this is simply great.
If I may put it bluntly
You're raising our birthrate.
Please, doctor, now we're homeless . . .
But you'll have a bed somewhere
So best put your feet up, moan less
And force yourself to grin and bear.
You'll make a simply splendid little mummy
Producing cannon fodder from your tummy
That's what your body's for, and you know it, what's more
And it's laid down by law
And now get this straight:
You'll soon be a mother, just wait.

But, doctor, no job or dwelling:
My man would find kids the last straw . . .
No, rather a new compelling
Objective to work for.

But, doctor . . . really, Frau Griebel
I ask myself what this means
You see, our State needs people
To operate our machines.
You'll make a simply splendid little mummy
Producing factory fodder from your tummy
That's what your body's for, and you know it, what's more
And it's laid down by law
And now get this straight:
You'll soon be a mother, just wait.

But, doctor, there's such unemployment . . .
I can't follow what you say.
You're all out for enjoyment
then grumble at having to pay.
If we make a prohibition
You bet we've a purpose in mind.
Better recognise your condition
And once you've agreed to put yourselves in our hands, you'll
        find
You're a simply splendid little mummy
Producing cannon fodder from your tummy
That's what your body's for, and you know it, what's more
And it's laid down by law
And now get this straight:
You'll soon be a mother, just wait.

Sonnets

A form that can be helpful to you as an emerging writer is the *sonnet* (meaning 'little song'), a poem of fourteen lines.

Traditionally sonnets are used as a vehicle for personal expression, either in love or as a tribute to a friend. They are intimate, and allow you to develop and explore a single idea.

American grandfather

Vitality in old men is attractive:
in Riverdale, I met Peggy's grandad,
his sleek white hair and black suit
no cover for the thin, electric body.
He works a six-day week in Brooklyn,
has no time to compromise.
Drives the New York streets
like a teenager in his silver Chevrolet.
He knows the insect world as intelligent,
more beautiful than the city's
concrete honeycomb; strives unwittingly
to get free of his historical cocoon.
He throws you with bird-logic,
tilts at the Quixotic moon.

Apart from 'cocoon' and 'moon' and the end, that sonnet about an eccentric character living in New York doesn't rhyme. Unrhymed sonnets are a modern variation on the sonnet form; traditionally, they have been written in 'Shakespearian' rhyming pattern – *ababcdcdefefgg* – or in the 'Italian' pattern (so called because the sonnet was introduced to England from Italy) – *abbaabba cdccdc*. In the Italian type, the break between the first eight lines (the *octave*) and the last six (the *sestet*) is marked, and often signifies a turning point in the poem; whereas the final couplet (see p.62) in the Shakespearian type tends to sum up the previous twelve lines:

Shall I compare thee to a summer's day?
Thou art more lovely and more temperate:
Rough winds do shake the darling buds of May,
And summer's lease hath all too short a date:
Sometime too hot the eye of heaven shines,
And often is his gold complexion dimm'd;
And every fair from fair sometime declines,
By chance, or nature's changing course, untrimm'd;
But thy eternal summer shall not fade,
Nor lose possession of that fair thou owest;
Nor shall death brag thou wander'st in his shade,
When in eternal lines to time thou growest;
    So long as men can breathe, or eyes can see,
    So long lives this, and this gives life to thee.

William Shakespeare

Sonnet XXXVIII

First time he kissed me, he but only kissed
The fingers of this hand wherewith I write;
And ever since, it grew more clean and white,
Slow to world-greetings, quick with its 'Oh, list,'
When the angels speak. A ring of amethyst
I could not wear here, plainer to my sight,
Than that first kiss. The second passed in height
The first, and sought the forehead, and half missed,
Half falling on the hair. O beyond meed!
That was the chrism of love, which love's own crown,
With sanctifying sweetness, did precede.
The third upon my lips was folded down
In perfect, purple state; since when, indeed,
I have been proud and said, 'My love, my own.'

Elizabeth Barrett Browning

Here are two sonnets written by students in school:

Solitude

I shiver slightly standing there, entombed by
The cold crisp high-vaulted air.
Above a kaleidoscope of richly coloured glass
Depicts far away biblical scenes; strange, silent saints.
The hardness and the brightness of the light
Spills over coldly embracing the stone floor,
But not reaching me with its touch,
Not softly stroking my skin with its warm glow.
And beyond me, beyond the window, what is there?
A larger loneliness of crowded empty streets,
Of faces vaguely glimpsed and soon forgot,
Of those known well and yet not known at all,
A quick-paced indulgent dance of youth.
Yet underneath a deep desire for something else, something real.

Sarah Ironside

The room is full, yet her thoughts are her own,
Head bent in silent contemplation.
He knows she's there, and watches her alone,
Then laughter shatters her concentration.
She lifts her head and her eyes sweep the room,
Calm sea under a gentle April morn.
Pale and misty, each a luminous moon,
Light and clear, a frost at an icy dawn.
Their lustre moves him, innocent power,
One liquid glance can stir in him new life.
Self conscious, her blushing face bends lower,
A shadow of a smile upon her mouth.
He is her moon, her eyes the restless tide,
Reflecting the light she cannot keep inside.

Frances Robson

Writing about oneself

Writing about oneself did not become a fashion in English literature until Wordsworth finished his long autobiographical poem *The Prelude* in 1806, addressed to his friend, Coleridge. It was clearly important to Wordsworth to feel that he was indeed talking to someone in his poem – someone he could trust and pour out his innermost feelings to.

In this early passage from the poem, he remembers where he grew up and his life before he was nine:

> Fair seed-time had my soul, and I grew up
> Foster'd alike by beauty and by fear;
> Much favour'd in my birthplace, and no less
> In that beloved Vale to which, erelong,
> I was transplanted. Well I call to mind
> ('Twas at an early age, ere I had seen
> Nine summers) when upon the mountain slope
> The frost and breath of frosty wind had snapp'd
> The last autumnal crocus, 'twas my joy
> To wander half the night among the Cliffs
> And the smooth Hollows, where the woodcocks ran
> Along the open turf. In thought and wish
> That time, my shoulder all with springes hung,
> I was a fell destroyer. On the heights
> Scudding away from snare to snare, I plied
> My anxious visitation, hurrying on,
> Still hurrying, hurrying onward; moon and stars
> Were shining o'er my head; I was alone,
> And seem'd to be a trouble to the peace
> That was among them. Sometimes it befel
> In these night-wanderings, that a strong desire
> O'erpower'd my better reason, and the bird
> Which was the captive of another's toils
> Became my prey; and, when the deed was done
> I heard among the solitary hills
> Low breathings coming after me, and sounds
> Of undistinguishable motion, steps
> almost as silent as the turf they trod.

A useful way to begin writing about your life is to try to tell the entire story of your life in a poem about as long as the one that follows:

A short story of my life

I was born in Dulwich Hospital on 3rd August
1955.
I was to be the last of five children
for my Mum and Dad.
I have 3 sisters and 1 brother.

I remember a lot of the good times of my
childhood, like holidays and Christmas
when all the family were together and happy.

But as I got older
I realised the family was not as happy
as I thought.
We were always fighting between ourselves.

I spent a lot of weekends at my aunt's house.
I went on Friday night
And came home Sunday night.
I went to get away from my brother and sisters.

I was 13 when I met my first boy friend.
He introduced me to his friend Tony
after three months,
I started to go out with him.
He gave me a lot of happy times.
When I was fifteen my life changed
I was going to have Tony's baby.
I felt on top of the world and happier than I
have ever felt.
When I told my parents
they looked down on me.
I don't know why, because they helped my two
sisters.
They kept talking about abortion and adoption.
I did not want either,
I wanted my baby.

I was 16 by the time the baby was born.
I had a lot of trouble with the birth.
She was born feet first,
you would think my mother would help me
understand.

But they did not seem to care.
I lived at home with my baby and my family
for 3 months and then I got married to Tony on
the 19th February 1972.
We lived in two rooms above his mother.
It was hard but we were together.
Two years later I was expecting another baby.
My two rooms were too small
and they were in very bad condition
not fit for a baby.
So I did all I could
to get a good home for us all.

I was in hospital for a rest
because I was worried about my home and my
baby when one night at visiting time my husband
came in with a letter.
It was to say we were to view a flat.
It was lovely.
We took the flat and moved in.
A few months later our second baby was born.

Now I have been married for nearly 4 years
I have two beautiful daughters
and a lovely husband.
I am so happy now.
I have had to fight for everything I have got
but I don't regret it.
We don't have much money but we are happy.

Kathryn Wilkinson

Then, when you have charted your life up to now, you could go back and concentrate on
particular moments or places or people that are important to you . . .

Playing

(for Beth, Adam and Corky)

Lawless places
The backyard
The edge of the woods
Pretending to be horses
Clearing paths first
Setting up jumps
And then running through
From one back house to the next.
There was one tree
Among the brush and bushes
With a flat, round rock at the base
A starting point.

One little brother
Sat on the side of the house
Where one neighbor meets another
Playing with parts of coffee pots.
His mom would buy him
Percolaters
Tin pot – cup – strainer – stand
Pulling them apart and putting together.

While in the backyards we would run
Jumping, cantering, a trot, a gallop –

The front lawn football fields
For touchdowns
And running passes
The streets
For rollerskating
Bumped and high
A skate key
On a dirty string necklace
In a jar somewhere
On the kitchen table
Or on mother's desk
Lost again.
Then we would have to share
Trapping our feet
In metal clasps
Lifting heavy steps
To grind over paved streets

And in one, small, dirt patch
Between the hedges that edged the driveway
Grew the only flowers I could ever identify,
Tulips.

April Ivy Krassner

Childhood reverie

Great Grandma Butts's house
White wainscotted walled kitchen
Crunchy linoleum
A solitary red hand pump for water
Stark, bare, primitive yesteryear.

The musky, moldy, damp smell
I could taste in every room
Breathing through my mouth
For moments of escape.

I lurked through the rooms
Waist-high in chattering aunts and uncles
Dodging monster claws on furniture
Seeking out my hiding place, my special place
The cathedral.

Great Grandma's organ room
So reverently I'd enter and
Stroke the ceiling-high organ
Wonderstruck by the dark rich treasure
Hand-carved spires and turrets
Yellowed ivory keys
Stops to pull out, push in.

I'd quietly slide onto the bench
Flip out the bellow pedals
Pump, pump, pump, pump
Anticipating the first sigh of sound
Aching to get out.

And nightmare horrors on second floor
Round holes cut through to downstairs
For heat to come up
Worry, worry that I'd fall through.

Worse yet, the ominous outhouse
And my tears as I sat there
Wondering if snakes
Would bite my bottom.

Great Grandma Butts's house
I slinked into the car
Crouched in a corner
And quietly awaited our arrival.

Camille Koepnick

Nikki-Rosa

childhood rememberances are always a drag
if you're Black
you always remember things like living in Woodlawn
with no inside toilet
and if you become famous or something
they never talk about how happy you were to have your mother
all to yourself and
how good the water felt when you got your bath from one of those
big tubs that folk in chicago barbecue in
and somehow when you talk about home
it never gets across how much you
understood their feelings
as the whole family attended meetings about Hollydale
and even though you remember
your biographers never understand
your father's pain as he sells his stock
and another dream goes
and though you're poor it isn't poverty that
concerns you
and though they fought a lot
it isn't your father's drinking that makes any difference
but only that everybody is together and you
and your sister have happy birthdays and very good christmasses
and I really hope no white person ever has cause to write about me
because they never understand Black love is Black wealth and they'll
probably talk about my hard childhood and never understand that
all the while I was quite happy

Nikki Giovanni

True grit

Throughout this book there are references to, and examples of, drafting. Most established poets use this technique to help them arrive at exactly what they want to say. It enables them to try out ideas, discover the rhythms of what they want to say, shape their statement and leave out anything that doesn't 'fit'.

Sometimes it is a long process; and sometimes other people can do it better than the writer him- or herself, because of being more 'distant' from the poem, and more 'objective'.

Here is a set of drafts that a fourth year girl worked on independently of her teacher. What he saw in the work she presented at school was only the tip of an iceberg of writing and rewriting.

It provides an excellent model of the kind of technique and determination you can use when composing.

1   Unformed anecdote

Holiday, went shopping for Mum, long way road from pier to town,
wouldn't go on ferry because yobos on it, had to walk all way round,
longer than I expected, desperation, no-one in sight, only my Howards
to keep me company, kept going, I couldn't give up, I was being silly,
got to other side, relief, went up ally, no-one there, scared, no-one
to talk to, went up another allie, found shops, co-op, bought some
apples and spoke to someone, relief. Wandered round village. Now, I
dreaded going back to that lonely pier, no-one there only dots for people
There were two chinease people, one pushing a baby, I smiled, relief
again, I'd made contact with som I got back, I couldn't find Mum or
Dad or brother. Panick yet again. This was so silly, I didn't need
anyone to takto, but obviously did.
 I saw a familiar shape walking up the pier, Dad. All over. I'm never
going to walk that again, Dad.
Why, it was just too long! to be on my

[handwritten insertions:]
I was beginning to feel there wasn't any town here
there is a town here after all.
to
It seemed there were no real people here
some colours

[handwritten:]

Homework
Story or poem.
Work on it.

2   The pier

An errand I was sent on,
On that thursday morning
The pier was long and lonely
~~No one for company, only~~
Only my thoughts for company.
'It seems' my thoughts said
~~It seemed~~ there ~~was~~ nothing
nothing apart from me & as I wal   my thoughts
~~no people or shops on that pier~~
                    this bare pier
~~As I~~ walkeding along ~~that cold hard~~
I reached my destination,
After loosing my way in a maze
unfamiliar to me.
                      many
I found a shop and ~~with lots of~~
                   ~~bought people~~
being busy with shopping
~~moving around~~ and talking
~~'All is not 'It seems' I said to my thoughts~~
                          'you were quite wrong',
~~you were quite wrong'~~

~~I bought~~ And I bought the apples

3   All is not what it seems

I was sent to buy apples
   the flat hard
on ~~Thursday~~ morning
   pier
The ~~seemed~~ long and lonely, almost never ending
                           unending length
as I ~~walked along it~~ it's ter nothingness
with only my thoughts to keep me company.
It seems, they told me, 'that there are no people'
Living here apart from you and me.'
~~I stupidly bothered my thoughts~~ them
~~I didn't want to; but'~~   ~~my thoughts~~
                          they were like dark puddles I
                          didn't want to step into
and walked up the naked pier
I reached my destination
After loosing my way,
And my thoughts
ln panic
I found a shop ~~with many~~ people standing
~~Shopping and talking~~ Real people
'It seems' I said to my thoughts happily 'you
were quite wrong!'
~~And I bought the apples.~~

130

4   A different start

On a very
hard morning
I carried on walking up
the weather scrubbed boards until
I reached the end.
~~I lost~~ After losing myself
and my thoughts
In panic
I found myself in a shop
~~It was warm and cosy~~
~~With mothers buying apples and bread~~
~~Such reliable~~
~~'It seems' I said to myself~~
~~'You were quite wrong'~~

                    sweet
              soft
It was warm & ~~reliable~~ comforting
With things that never changed
So reliable...
'It seems,' I said to myself
'You were quite wrong.'

5   Trying an edit

~~I was sent to buy apple~~
I carried on walking up
the weather scrubbed boards, until
I reached the end.
After loosing myself
And my thoughts
In panic
I found a shop
~~It seemed to It was warm inside~~
~~from the body heat the people~~
Inside ~~the people made it warm~~
the people made it warm
I felt safe - blanketed ~~with warmth~~
~~It~~ 'it seems,' I gasped to myself
'You were quite wrong'

✓ Want an image not a statement   131

6 **All is not what it seems**

~~An errand~~ I was sent to buy apples
on that Thursday morning.
The pier was long and ~~never~~ lonely
never ending as I walked along
it with only my thoughts to keep
me company.
~~'It seems there is nothing here~~
~~apart~~
It seems' my thoughts told me 'that
there are ~~is~~ no people living here ~~nothing else here apart~~
from you and me!'
I believed my thoughts and carried
on up the bare pier.
I found a shop.
~~It was fixed firmly~~
~~on the corner of the street~~
~~It was~~
Fixed like a cottage loaf
firmly on the corner.
Warm from the oven

Here is the final version:

All is not what it seems

I was sent to buy apples
On that flat, hard morning
The pier seemed long, lonely and endless
as I walked through its nothingness
Only the two of us
me and my thoughts
'It seems' they told me 'that you and I
are the only people here.'
My thoughts were like rooms
I was forbidden to enter.
I carried on walking up
the weather scrubbed boards
I reached the end
After losing myself and my thoughts
In panic.
I found a shop
Fixed like a cottage loaf
Firmly on the corner
Warm from the oven.
'It seems,' I said to myself
'You were quite wrong!'

Sione Watts

About writing poems 4

Shush – Mum's writing

Sit down be quiet read a book
Don't you dare to speak or look
Shush Mum's writing

She's left the dishes in the sink
All she does is sit and think
Shush Mum's writing

Nothing for dinner nowt for tea
And all she ever says to me is
Shush Mum's writing

But what's all this Mum's wrote a book
Why not buy one have a look
No need to shush now we can shout
And tell our friends about
MUM'S WRITING

Maureen Burge

Acknowledgments

The author would like to thank the following for permission to print their poems: Rachel Allen, Elizabeth Ashurst, Stephen Bell, Jane Bertram, Karen Carlton, Collin Cameron, Andrew Clark, Andrew Craig, Keith Dearlove, Karen Fitzgerald, A. Gardner, Debbie la Haye, John Hodder, Rachel Hutton, Sarah Ironside, Margaret Jay, Sarah Jane Kayser, Kathryn Kent, Phillip King, Camille Koepnick, April Krassner, Gavin Long, Danny Marriott, Julie Nendick, James O'Neill, Dean Osborne, Ian Parsons, David Pipes, Trevor Pye, Tracy Radley, Lenny Rhodes, Frances Robson, Katy Robson, Lisa Salsbury, Nigel Skinner, Nicola Stewart, Samantha Sweeney, Beverley Tizzard, Craig Turnock, Sione Watts, Tracey White, Gary Wilson, Jenny Wren, Robert Wright; and the following for their help: Jane Austen-Smith, Edith Ervin, Angela Fisher, John Foggin, Anna Harland, David Harland, Alasdair Macdonald, Uist Macdonald, David Strickland, and especially Dodi Beardshaw.

The author and publishers would like to thank the following for permission to use copyright material: Harper & Rowe, Publishers, Inc., for 'My hobby' from *Where the Sidewalk Ends; the Poems and Drawings of Shel Silverstein*, © 1974 by Shel Silverstein; Oxford University Press for 'The ever-touring Englishmen' and 'What is man's body?' from *Folk Songs of the Maikal Hills* by Elwin & Hivale, and for 'Wind' from *A History of Classical Malay Literature* by Winstedt, and for extracts from *The Pillowbook of Sei Shonagon* trans. and ed. Ivan Morris, © Ivan Morris 1967; to Secker and Warburg Ltd. for 'Very brief thoughts on the letter M' from *Notes of a Clay Pigeon* by Miroslav Holub; The Menard Press and Harry Matthews for 'ABC'; University of California Press for 'How the gallows child remembers the names of the months' from *Gallows Songs* by Christian Morgenstern; Edition Hansjörg Mayer for 'Apfel/Wurm' by Reinhard Döhl from *The Anthology of Concrete Poetry*, ed. Williams; Carcanet New Press Ltd. for 'Message Clear', 'Archives', 'Shaker Shaken', 'The computer's first dialect poems' and the extract from 'Canedolia' from *Poems of Thirty Years* by Edwin Morgan, and for 'Film put in backwards' by Günter Kunert, trans. Christopher Middleton, from *East German Poetry*, ed. Michael Hamburger; the author for 'Glasgow 5 March 1971', 'Fallin Stirlingshire October 1970' and 'Innsbruck July 1971' from *Instamatic Poems* by Edwin Morgan; Anvil Press Poetry Ltd. for extracts from *The Golden Apple* by Vasko Popa; Doubleday and Company Inc., for 'The Killer', © 1972 by Jerome Rothenberg from *Shaking the Pumpkin* by Jerome Rothenberg; Stella Johns for 'The day I wrote a poem'; Professor C R Bawden for 'The 'word' of a wolf encircled by the hunt'; The Owen Estate and Chatto & Windus Ltd. for 'The letter' from *War Poems and Others* by Wilfred Owen, ed. Dominic Hibberd; Monthly Review Press for 'Hunger', 'Dream', 'The winds' and 'Moon' from *The Great Zoo* by Nicolas Guillén, © 1972 by Robert Marquez; Heinemann Educational Books for 'Touch' by Hugh Lewin from *Poets to the People*, ed. Barry Feinberg; Faber and Faber Ltd. for 'A cranefly in September' and 'The warm and the cold' from *Season Songs* by Ted Hughes, and for 'Love poem' from *Terry Street* by Douglas Dunn; Writers and Readers Publishing Co-operative Society Ltd. for the extract from *About Looking* by John Berger; Bogle-l'Ouverture Publications Ltd. for the extract from *Dread Beat and Blood* by Linton Johnson; *Race Today* for 'Sonny's Lettah' from *Inglan is a Bitch* by Linton Johnson; Fred Williams for his poem 'Harrassment'; Tom Leonard for his poem 'this is thi six a clock news'; International Creative Management, Inc., for 'I seem to be . . . but I really am . . .' and 'I seem to be but I am a . . .' from *Wishes Lies and Dreams* by Kenneth Koch; The ILEA English Centre and the author for 'South side' by James Smith from *City Lines: Poems by London School Students*; Hutchinson Publishing Group Ltd. for 'I'm glad to be up and about' by Taufiq Rafat and 'An un-African breakfast' by Joe de Graft, both from *Many People Many Voices*, ed. Norman Hidden and Amy Hollins; Souvenir Press Ltd. for the extract from *Reflections of a Clyde-built Man* by Jimmy Reid; Times Newspapers Ltd. for 'Visit in the Garden of Eden ends with an apple fall' by David Blundy from *The Sunday Times*, 10 October 1982; George Allen & Unwin for 'Roadmenders' song' from *Songs of the Forest*; Présence Africaine for 'Africa' by David Diop from *Coups de Pilon* (Paris, 1956); Methuen Ltd. for 'The ballad of paragraph 218' by Bertolt Brecht; Bristol Broadsides (co-op) Ltd. and the author for 'Shush – Mum's writing' by Maureen Burge.

Every effort has been made to contact owners of copyright material, but in some cases this has not proved possible. The publishers would be glad to hear from any further copyright owners of material reproduced in *Into Poetry*.

The publishers are grateful to the following for the loan of photographic material in this book: Barnaby's Picture Library (p. 54, left); Popperfoto (p. 79).